D0266351

FLUFFY DICE

for
Elizabeth and Philip
with lots of love
from

Nigel   *June '87*

To Victor Lewis-Smith
and
Jan Strachen

FLUFFY DICE

NIGEL FORDE

ILLUSTRATED BY DEBBIE RYDER

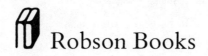 Robson Books

Thanks are owed to *The Listener*, in whose pages
'Sir John Laments His Influence' have appeared.

First published in Great Britain in 1987 by Robson Books Ltd,
Bolsover House, 5–6 Clipstone Street, London W1P 7EB.

Copyright © 1987 Nigel Forde.

British Library Cataloguing in Publication Data

Forde, Nigel
    Fluffy dice and other 'midweek' verse.
    I. Title
    821'.914   PR6056.066/

ISBN 0-86051-437-4

All rights reserved. No part of this publication may be
reproduced, stored in a retrieval system, or transmitted in
any form or by any means, electronic, mechanical,
photocopying, recording or otherwise, without the prior
permission in writing of the publishers.

Printed in Great Britain by Billing & Sons Ltd.,
Worcester.
Typeset in Great Britain by Bookworm Typesetting,
Manchester.

Contents

MIDWEEKENDINGS

Part 2: XENOPHOBIA–ZOIC

Foreword

'We're having a poet, every week,' said the previous producer of 'Midweek' one day. 'He's quite modern. He'll actually write a poem during the programme. You know, something tough, reactive. Off the wall.' I felt apprehensive. This particular producer, talented as he was, had shown a mischievous tendency to invite on to the programme the sort of people who make Radio 4 listeners nervous (and Radio 4 presenters, too). I'd get into the office on a Tuesday and be told that one of the guests was going to bang a nail up his nose, live on the air; that another had 'promised to keep it clean, but might need controlling', and that yet another was going to perform an Alternative Cabaret turn with a block of ice and a blowtorch. This was all very well, since each guest only came once; the promise of an 'off-the-wall' spontaneous poet every single week was distinctly unnerving. But 'His name's Nigel Forde,' said Victor commandingly. 'And he's booked.'

I can't remember the moment when I stopped worrying, and became a passionate Forde partisan. It can't have taken long: week after week, Nigel arrived, quiet and dark and smiling, with a neatly-typed poem on a set theme to read at the beginning, and a scruffy little black notebook in which to write his 'instant poem' on the week's guests. The opening themes were sometimes gentle, predictable Radio 4 stuff – springtime, or Christmas, or holidays; sometimes they reflected Nigel's own deepest preoccupations and hates – like Fluffy Dice or sloppy language; sometimes showed signs of being inspired by the producer's alternative sense of humour. I think it was one of these, in fact, that finally reassured me that I was safe with Nigel. The theme given was President Reagan's abdominal operation; I asked worriedly, 'It's not going to be tasteless, is it?', and it wasn't. Nigel Forde is not capable of tastelessness. He can be fierce, quirky, original, or deep, but nothing he writes is devoid of feeling and truth. When the Instant poems get him floored, with no witty theme coming to hand, he takes refuge in outrageous puns. If he ventures an insult, it is such a good one that the object of it beams appreciatively and forgets to be offended.

Once reassured, I sat back happily to enjoy the Forde way with language and images. He described his domestic poems once as 'Giles cartoons in verse', and there is something of vintage Giles about them: a sort of broad comedy founded on understanding, with a good eye for the small frustrations of life. Like the onset of winter, when:

> . . . *the bland and biddable butter suddenly*
> *Savages the bread.*

There is romanticism, too, although he sends it up like a true Englishman: my favourite poem title is 'English Angels Smiled with English Smiles upon the Scenery, Which is why the Whole of England's Like a Garden in a Deanery.'

We get a lot of letters at 'Midweek': about half of them now demand copies of Nigel's latest poem, or photographs of the great man himself. One lady sent her picture, with a fearful orange topknot, explaining in verse that she had been so rapt with

> '*Nigel's wit beyond compare*
> *That I quite forgot I was dyeing my hair.*'

All these correspondents have said that they wish they could get Nigel in hard covers. Here is their answer. Enjoy it.

L. P., MARCH 1987

FLUFFY DICE

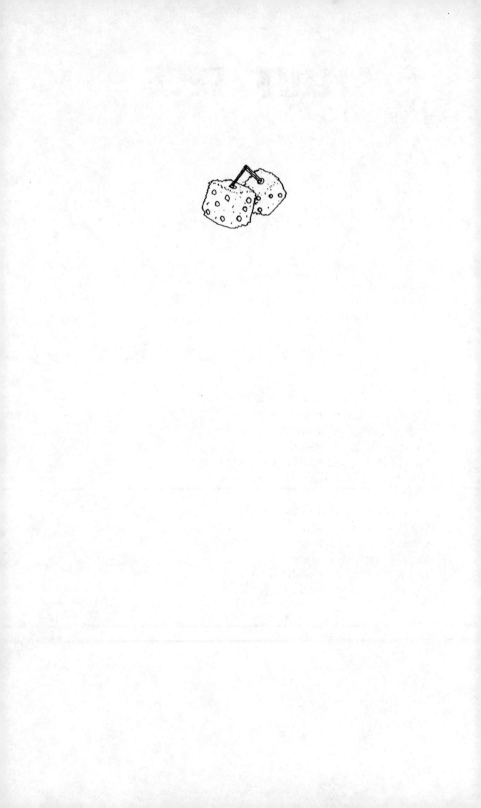

Part 1:
ANGST–BROADS

Fluffy Dice or Neuroses in Bloom

In a world overhung by the Nuclear Threat,
A world of a million woes,
Where man's little more than red tooth and red claw
And injustice and poverty grows,
It's odd how it's always the *littlest* things
That really get up your nose.

I can't stand painted yellow lines
On the streets of an ancient city –
A double dose of the really gross
Council-approved graffiti;
I don't like a man who's just met a girl
And begins by calling her 'sweetie'.

Or supermarket trolleys that
Go any way but straight;
Or anything you have to buy
In plastic packs of eight;
But fluffy dice on dashboards –
That's the thing I really hate!

I don't like the singers on comedy shows
(All dry-ice, or soft-focus with leaves)
I don't like sweaty men in shirts
With silver bands on their sleeves;
Or Barratt estates or Tupperware plates
Or split infinitives.

I hate to hear pop from another room –
That ineluctable 4/4
That sheds its upper partials
And comes thudding through the floor;
But fluffy dice that hang in cars
Is what I most abhor.

I hate the way rain blows in your face
Whichever way you look;
And smokeless zones and ansafones
And dog-ears in a book,
And toenails on the bathroom floor
And houses called 'The Nook'.

I hate those apostrophes they put
On words in burger bars –
You know: Fish 'n' Chips 'n' Ham 'n' Eggs;
I hate Russell Grant and Stars;
But I'll tell you what I hate the most of all –
It's fluffy dice in cars!

I don't like sportsmen who never use adverbs
But always 'play good' and 'run quick';
I dislike the pith in tangerines,
Warm loo seats, and the slick
Smile of a politician when
He should be looking sick.

I don't like TV series that
Deny the human brain,
Or the tsk-tatta-tsk-tatta-tsk-tatta-tsk
Of the walkman on the train;
But the fluffy dice that hang in cars
Are driving me insane.

So, when the revolution comes
And the world is put to rights,
You can deal with the crooks, the depraved, the corrupt,
The varieties of vice;
But leave *me* the man who's covered his van
With little fluffy dice!

The Ballad of the Baby-Sitter

She picked me up at seven o'clock
In her husband's company car,
With the fluffy dice on the dashboard
And the stale smell of middle tar.

She drove me back, in second gear,
To 12A Redshank Walk.
(That's just beyond Starling and Wheatear Close
Before they meet Sparrowhawk.)

The reproduction coach-lamp shed
Soft pink on the gathering gloom;
The carpet snapped at my ankles
As I walked to the living room.

I knew what she'd say, when I saw the gold–
Fish bowl with the Lego scum,
The biro-blistered wallpaper,
The plastic Wendy-slum,

The jig-saw confetti, the Sindy clothes,
The acres of moulded plastic
And a dozen dolls in debauched disarray
For want of efficient elastic;

The kitchen like a mountain range
Of grease-thick pans and bowls
And Pyrex dishes welded to
Old stews and casseroles.

And she said: 'I've had such a day today!
All this – well, I tried to get through it.
But promise me, my dear – no, please!
Don't feel you *have* to do it!'

She introduced me to her brood:
A girl with hair like Titian,
A grim, gross baby with a face
Like a pre-war politician,

And a sullen boy who had every toy
That's ever been modelled on war;
And a Dr Who quilt and a Dr Who lamp
And a Dr Who rug on the floor.

Then she left with her husband in
A nostril-numbing haze
Of Tweed and Brut and dry-cleaned suit
And a trichological glaze.

The bookshelf offered Cookson, Christie,
Some Reader's Digest Condensings
And a specialist volume concerned with the art
Of larch-lap and chestnut fencings.

I needn't have worried: as soon as I'd finished
The tidying, washing and cleaning
The Titian-head wailed for a bedtime story
The baby started screaming.

So I read an exciting tale involving
Peter and Jane and a dog;
And put another nappy on
The bald and bawling frog.

I removed the sullen boy from the fridge
And beamed him up the stairs,
But not before he'd exterminated
A mousse and eight éclairs

Then I read about kittens and rabbits and ducks
And some sybarite called Mr Happy;
I cleared up the sick in the sullen boy's room
And changed another nappy.

The stories stopped at 11.03
When she finally went to sleep.
Then the baby woke up at 11.14.
Right. Back to the kittens and sheep . . .

Come quarter to one I'd run out of nappies
Exhausted the farmyard and zoo
And scrubbed Tom Baker so many times
That you couldn't tell he was Who.

By the time I heard their car draw up
With a smug, smooth creak of leather
I was dribbling and babbling of green fields:
A man at the end of his tether

I'm not sure what possessed me, quite
But I twisted a couple of bolsters
And laid them out alongside a gun
From one of the sullen boy's holsters.

I found one of those very lifelike dolls
And propped it on the stair;
I bandaged its limbs with elastoplast
And rubbed ketchup into its hair.

And as I write, two men in white
Are coming to see me again;
If I'm good, they'll read me a story about
A dog, and Peter, and Jane . . .

English Angels Smiled with English Smiles upon the Scenery, Which is why the Whole of England's Like a Garden in a Deanery

An Englishman, an Englishman
Is a glorious thing to be;
He's farther up the ladder
And he's mother of the free;
He's drawn the winning ticket in the
Birthright lottery.

The Englishman is a decent man,
What he knows is worth the knowing;
He takes his ease beneath family trees
With port and sherry flowing;
He's nobody's fool: prep., public school,
Then Keble for the rowing.

Let other nations rant and rave,
Gabble and fight and scream;
An Englishman is not so easily
Driven to an extreme –
He taps his chin with a forefinger
If he needs to let off steam.

He's Gawain, Raleigh, Robin Hood,
He's Elgar, Drake and Scott,
With a touch of Ian Botham and
Of Roger Moore a lot;
Disguised, of course, in spectacles
And growing bald and squat.

Life is hard (a fact to which
The Englisman will alert you),
What's pleasant is bad and nothing's worthwhile
Unless it's likely to hurt you;
The world is a moral gymnasium built
To train him into virtue.

An Englishman thrives on Plutarch's 'Lives'
Tradition and History;
He always takes the broader view
And a second cup of tea,
And *still* has a deep, devouring dread
Of decimal currency.

An Englishman, oh an Englishman
Will always take it in
Good part, good faith, or stages,
Or even on the chin.
Why, Nelson's blood flows in his veins!
– You can see where it got in.

An Englishman likes to compromise,
For nothing's cut and dried;
'Great wits', he's fond of quoting, 'are
To madness near allied';
So his thoughts are middle-of-the-road
And he drives on either side.

The Englishman can be hated, mocked,
Reviled or caricatured –
He'll turn the other cheek; just one thing
Sticks in his throat: good Lord!
He may be an Englishman at home,
He's a *foreigner* abroad!

Oh, the Englishman's home is his castle, still,
Though the moat has turned to a bog,
And any airs it gave itself
Have thickened to a fog;
Now a dim light falls on its peeling walls;
There's a smell of unwashed dog.

Where is the world of the Englishman,
Predictable and tidy?
The centre cannot hold, there's nothing
Left but bona fide;
Sic transit gloria mundi, Tuesday,
Wednesday, Thursday, Friday.

The Harmless, Necessary Cat

A poet always runs the risk –
However great his skills –
Of saying what's been said before:
'Sweet spring! . . .' 'Santanic mills . . .',
Or parking himself on Wordsworth's double
Yellow daffodils.

Some writers have staked unassailable claims,
Like Melville on the whale,
Blake Blake on the Tiger Tiger
And Keats on the nightingale;
Lawrence, of course, owns snake and bat;
Hardy's oxen are not for sale.

Ted Hughes has all the British rights
On everything else that goes
On four legs, wings or dorsal fins –
Pigs, otters, bulls and crows,
Owls, salmon, swifts, pike, jaguar; hawks
In rain or in repose.

Moles? William Horwood. Rabbits? Adams.
O'Brien has done the rat;
So – pace T. S. Eliot –
'Old Possum' and all that,
I'm going to have another go.
At the humble, household cat.

What can one say that's not been said
About the feline race?
Genghis Khan's compassion mixed
With Margot Fonteyn's grace;
An Anglo-Catholic conscience in
A Calvinistic face.

An old, brown sack with one open eye,
A rug wrapped round a purr,
A splinter of night, a trick of the light,
A professional amateur;
A slit in the dark, first one on the ark,
A complete surprise – with fur.

Cats 'fearfully o'ertrip the dew'
Like Thisbe in the play;
Hate water, toddlers, Hoovers, being
Expected to obey.
They have a limpet's obstinacy;
Cats sulk or rule – OK!

They have nine lives, the proverb says,
And there's always nine to go;
They like to feel their status and
To keep the status quo;
A cross between a diplomat
And the local Mafioso.

They say cats are stand-offish – well,
They're quite sit-onnish too,
But there's an awful lot of rubbish talked
Of cats, that is not true;
They say they mutilate – they don't:
They mew till half-past two.

A kitten is a mobile brooch,
A bracelet on the wrist
Its mother will teach it to become
A true misanthropist;
What to know and how to flow
Through gaps that don't exist.

But never patronize a cat;
Don't make it look foolish, or
You'll pay for it when, on a certain day,
Through a normal kitchen door,
The tiger in him comes padding, padding,
On soft tons of paw.

Sir John Laments his Influence

Far beyond the brickish suburbs
Gothic mansions stand alone,
Where Young Fogeys chide and chunter;
Not quite Aesthete, not quite Sloane.

Stooping men of five-and-twenty,
This the blood that England breeds:
Mild and male and undistinguished
In their careful Harris tweeds.

Through their dreadful sense of beauty,
Ruskin, royals and altar-glow,
Through dynasties and light refreshments
The horns of England faintly blow.

Not for them the fitted carpets,
Rock, the sixties, video;
Esther Rantzen, Bics and Biros,
Laurie Taylor, Joan Miró;

Oh give them Kipling, claret, castles,
Cricket on the village green;
And prints of Corpus in the study
Where slippered men drink Ovaltine.

Is croquet over? Draw the curtains,
Evensong is almost sung.
Ah! You fond and foolish Fogeys,
I feel chilly and grown young.

I was I, yet – God forbid it! –
Now I walk the earth again
In all these cosy Betjechildren
Growing into Betjemen.

Wishful Printing
or
Headlines we will Never See

Cheaper phone calls coming soon,
Rolf Harris sings in tune;
Local council plans with taste,
Civil servants move in haste;
Public wants more poetry,
Pound worth over thirty p;
Third World surpluses of food,
Mary Whitehouse models nude;
Stravinsky moving up the charts,
Government subsidizes Arts;
'Crossroads' starts employing actors,
Building scheme has no detractors;
B.R. promise seats for all,
No one shot in Donegal;
Full employment by mid-May,
No roadworks on Motorway;
Crime-rate falls to record Nought,
News item found in 'Sunday Sport';
Atomic weapons: world says 'No',
Little and Large in comedy show;
And two to end with (so you'll see
it *is* dream, not reality):
Lloyd-Webber writes his final song,
Politician says 'I'm wrong'.

Giving Up

Ash Wednesday, then; and here beginneth
Forty days of frustration,
As we all indulge in an orgy
Of righteous renunciation.

We're proof against our base desires,
Against temptation's power;
And cigarette sales in all the shops
Will fall – for at least an hour.

And alcohol will plead in vain,
We'll be solid, selfless, sober;
And there'll be no babies born at all
In November or October.

But, of course, it doesn't work like that:
If you give up nicotine
You just hide your fags in outlandish spots
Where they can't be smelt or seen.

Behind the books on the topmost shelf,
Or blu-tacked under chairs;
And there's funny lumps – has the carpet got mumps? –
At the second bend of the stairs.

You can plant your whisky in pots in the shed:
John Innes number 3
Will root your cuttings, or sow the seeds
Of a small hypocrisy.

But when you go out at eleven each night
– Just to see if it's good Comet weather –
And come back stinking of extra-strong mints,
They'll put two and two together.

It's just like New Year's Resolutions:
Spirit willing, but flesh so frail.
Better not to start at all
Than make a start and fail.

In fact, the Church has noticed this
And given its assent –
Some of the liberal clergy I know
Are thinking of giving up Lent.

But who will be giving up what, I wonder?
I've got a kind of a hunch
That the caterers at Westminster
Will give up serving leeks at lunch;

Mills and Boon are going to give up
Pandering to members of Mensa;
Princess Di will try to get by
Without dresses from Marks and Spencer;

Terry Wogan will give up being such
A shy, retiring soul;
And Mrs Thatcher may give up her job
For some kind of leadership role.

Patrick Moore is going to give up
His manner, so ponderous and slow;
'That's Life' may give up the ghost altogether
And stick with Esther and Co.

Benny Hill will give up his career
And break into comedy;
David Coleman is going to give up
His chair in philology.

And what about me? What shall I give up?
What *does* one renounce at such times?
Well, what can *any* poet give up
But his metre and his ability to make really vivid and
    impressive images which remain in the imagination.

I'm sorry! – After so many stanzas
With rhymes all falling pat,
It really was unforgiveable
To end my poem like I did and I promise not to do it again.

Ugly Ducklingesang

Who'll make a song for a gawky girl
With a kindly, freckled face?
A girl with elbows and acne,
Who sometimes wears a brace?

I'm not a tall and willowy waif,
Pre-Raphaelite and faint;
I'm not the sort composers court
Or painters want to paint;
I haven't got a milk-white skin,
I'm neither saint nor whore;
I'm the girl whom operas
And song-cycles ignore.

So who'll make a song for a gawky girl,
The plainest plain Jane Eyre?
A girl with elbows and acne
And a hint of facial hair?

Mozart's girls are pretty, pert
And elegantly wise;
Bizet's birds aren't lost for words
And Verdi's – damn their eyes! –
Can even look alluring
In tubercular demise;
Schubert, it is true, put
Country girls upon the scene,
But I haven't got the figure for
A Schöne Müllerin.

O please make a song for a gawky girl
Without a lot of poise;
A girl with elbows and acne
Who frightens off the boys.

Come, da Ponte, Hofmannstahl,
Come Heine, Goethe, Schiller –
I'll settle for an opera
Called 'Madam Caterpillar'.
Oh, where is there a place for me
In all Romantic fiction?
Or who can cure my more than chronic
Heroine addiction?
Who will take a girl like me
Serenade her, need her?
Come, Schumann, Schubert, Wolf and Brahms
And take me to your lieder.

No, there isn't a song for a gawky girl
Who longs for a tenor to die
With her name upon his final breath
And a tear in every eye.

There'll never be songs for a girl like me,
All freckles and feet, I know.
Perhaps Susanna and Donna Anna
Can wait till I'm sixteen . . . or so.

The State of the Art

You mothers, you who wade today
In nappies to the knee
And dream of three or four years hence
When school will set you free;
Be thankful now for what you have:
The worst is yet to be.
They may not learn to speak or write
When they start nursery;
They may not learn their tables, or
To count beyond, say, three;
But one thing's certain: Art and Craft
Will be compulsory,
And you're going to have models of rockets and boats,
Wigwams, the Roman Forum,
Piled on the fridge or the working-tops
Or hung where you can't ignore them;
And, once they start, they're going to come
In saecula saeculorum.
The unkindest cut is that *you* provide
The rubbish from which they're made –
Straws, a shoe-box, thirty milk-bottle tops –
Then they're brought *home* to be displayed,
And the kitchen's a cross between Madame Tussaud's,
The V and A and the Slade.
It wouldn't be so bad if just *one*
Were a vaguely visual treat;
But they show all the truth of a Tory promise,
The charm of an athlete's feet,
And the freshness and original wit
Of a 'Little and Large' repeat.
Now, Rupert, whose father lectures at
The University,

Walks home with thoughtful and solemn gait
Each day at half-past three,
With delicate abstracts bearing titles
Like 'Purple Construct III',
While that metre of wind-tugged paper
With a pair of boots below
Is Georgie, staggering mum-wards
With a masterpiece to show;
His little cheeks all flushed with pride,
His little eyes aglow.
And you know very well what you're going to find
When you get it home: a small
Black squiggle on the right, a red
Amoebic splodge – that's all;
And you have to reply 'That's *lovely*, George!'
And pin it on the wall.
It's not alone, of course; oh, no –
We're well past half-term now:
It joins the anorexic owl,
The underprivileged sow,
It joins the camp, contemptuous cat,
The slight and sloping cow;
It joins the 'Wind in the Willows' cast
(Four Swiss rolls with a leer);
The amphibious, cross-eyed centipede
That's labelled 'Brighton Pier',
And the wombat in a walkman that's
Supposed to be a deer.
What looks like parboiled platypus
Congealing in its fat,
Or an ultra close-up study of
A just-exploded rat,
Is Wayne da Vinci's way of showing
'Daddy in his Hat'.
They curl, turn brown and brittle
Daubed with gravy, fat and brie;

They're bespidered, bent or broken
But you can't – believe you me –
You *can't* just stick them in the bin:
They're friends. They're family.
And when you're in your dotage,
With your kids beyond the sea,
And a trembling neighbour comes to help
You spill some Earl Grey tea,
And you find an Old Norse on a vole-like horse
With a squint and reversible knee,
You'll fondly point with a creaking joint:
'George did that when he was three!'

George age 3

April Love

Who so old but cannot take
Their mind years back, to when
Spring was green and love was greener;
Then we lived; oh, then
Girls were definitely girls
And boys . . . first drafts for men.

When brown legs slid from tennis shorts,
When you breathed youth and all that in;
When a shadow of lace through a white school blouse
Curved on a shoulder of satin
Could almost stop you breathing through
The whole of double Latin.

And all the furtive notes you sent
Through a dumpy, acned squire,
In the courtly-love tradition
(Half Donne and half Desire)
Culminate in the date to which
You hardly dared aspire.

So – Amplex, clean shirt, deodorant,
Teeth, nails, nose-hairs; tip
A pint and a half of Old Spice on –
A kind of gamesmanship:
The duvet stuffing's coarser than
The down upon your lip.

Then, to the cinema. Dare you hold
Her hand in the monochrome gleam?
Yes, you. . . No. . . Yes, No. . . Yes you can: deep breath,
Now . . . glue your eyes on the screen,
And close your fingers round that sweet, soft,
Yielding, cool . . . ice-cream.

And on the way to see her home
You dawdle in the park,
Waiting till the shadows make it
Reasonably dark
So contact can be accident
Yet hands still find their mark.

And when they do, and she half-smiles
And turns – the moment's near;
Old Spice, White Mink and new-mown grass
Will always mean her and here;
And everything is loud and now
And miraculously clear.

The way her jawbone meets her throat,
Pale, smooth and sanctified;
The way her body gently taps
Her clothes, from the inside;
The way she closes her almond eyes
Just as your teeth collide.

'Oh sorry . . .' 'No!' 'I meant . . .' 'Don't worry,
Look, come here – like this . . .'
And sixteen years of wisdom guide
You gently to the kiss;
A kind of chaste, electric, breathless,
Preter-sexual bliss.

'I s'pose you . . .' 'No' 'What?' 'No, I've never
Kissed a boy before.'
The heart's wild ostinato beats
A sudden 7/4,
The earth jars on its axis and
The silent landscapes roar.

And on the bus you smile and smile
And hug the future tight;
And all the world is suddenly
Ablaze with April light;
And pigeons' wings beat in your blood
And everything is *right*.

You lock the door and hang the key
Behind the jotter-pad,
And creep upstairs in silence, past
Dull, dozing mum and dad,
And enter in your diary:
'Kissed Linda. Not too bad.'

Fugitive and Cloistered

It's eighty degrees on the running field
And ninety inside the tents;
The grass has been shorn like a vicarage lawn
For the track and field events;
School Sports Day has come round again –
All sacks and violence.

And the motto 'Sequor ut Attingam'
Is blazoned on the stairs;
The hall is full of greenery,
The sports field's full of chairs;
There's Elgar in assembly
And there's Kipling after prayers.

And fat boys queue at the medical room
With sudden and crippling doses
Of food-poisoning, 'flu, Legionnaire's Disease –
And matron diagnoses
Twelve severe cases of swinging the lead
Or Plumbi Pendulosis.

And the morning's lessons are all a farce
For the Classics master's desire
Is his yearly fun with the starting gun
(After 'Linden Lea' from the choir)
And half an hour in the games cupboard
With young Miss MacIntyre.

The headmaster makes his usual speech
While the governors drink warm hock
With one eye on the scholarship boards
And another on the clock;
And the children avoid their parents all day
In case they're a laughing-stock.

The junior section starts the fun
With a sort of race affair
Involving hoops and ribbons and buckets
And masters tearing their hair;
It's a cross between 'Happiest Days of your Life'
And 'Jeux Sans Frontières'.

There are shots being put all over the place
And runners plodding by,
(Oh, the aubergine face of the last in the race!)
And javelins in the sky;
A grand and gripping spectacle
Like watching wet paint dry.

The PA system belches and screams
From the back of the caretaker's Transit;
It's slightly more fun than the sports themselves
But nobody understands it;
It's as clear as a British Rail station announcer
Reading *The Guardian* in Sanskrit.

And everyone's running around with lists
And having no little success
In making confusion worse confounded;
There's a general air of stress
And five false starts in the relay – but they're due
To Miss MacIntyre's new tennis dress.

So – while World Cup actors get thousands of pounds
As a bonus for winning a game,
And transatlantic boatmen enjoy
Champagne and TV fame,
And Wimbledon *losers* earn more in an hour
Than Peter Hall has to his name,

What's young William's prize for the lower-school sprint?
A speech about 'doing your best',
A clap on the back, two house-points, a star
To stick on his athletics vest
And his name, misspelt, in the school magazine
Next to 'Third-year Trip to Trieste'.

The Convergence of the Twain

The flower-arranger was in at six
As dawn broke over the land;
The sexton trims yews and the verger reviews
The order of service, as planned;
For Linda is going to be married today
In the church of St Agnes the Bland.

Two hours to go. The bride's mother's hair
Is a dripping, peroxide mess;
The bathroom looks like what's left behind
After you've drained Loch Ness;
The toast's alight, Granny's shoes are too tight
And the dog's been sick on the dress.

Cousin Midge puts her make-up on
With the help of a local welder;
'Anaglypta might help a bit?'
Offers Auntie Esmerelda,
Not exactly an oil-painting herself –
Unless by Breughel the Elder.

An hour to go, and the bride's disappeared;
Her mother goes white first, then blue.
She's not in the bedroom, she's not downstairs,
She's not locked herself in the loo;
She's found in the loft, in her underwear, reading
Her bridesmaids *Winnie The Pooh*.

Ten minutes to go. The relations leave
Clutching their attitudes;
Some like Acrilanned icebergs in un-
Familiar latitudes;
Others in massive floral prints,
Dispensing platitudes.

The drive to the church is a dismal affair,
Windy, cold and wet;
And the coolness between families
Who've scarcely ever met
Isn't helped by the ushers who ask each guest
'Montague or Capulet?'

You could be forgiven, when hearing the organ,
For thinking your throat's been skinned;
For it makes, when pumped by the short, fat legs
Of the seriously undisciplined,
A rude, remote and reedy sound
Like an old gnat breaking wind.

The organist – there's no accurate term –
Is on loan from St Stephen the Martyr,
And recruiting more with each bar she plays;
Her version of Widor's Toccata
Sounds like Messiaen upside-down
Or a volume of Schoenberg's errata.

The organ churns. The bridegroom turns
To where *she* stands, uncertainly;
As strange as alone, as old as the stone,
And still just twenty-three;
And he thuds inside and his eyes grow wide
Like a child who says 'For me?'

Was this the girl who sucked her biro
All through double Latin?
Who copied his Chemistry, snubbed him at break
And did his cricket bat in?
This angel at the western door
Adrift in a cloud of satin?

Let uncles make videos, choirs bleat,
And assorted nieces scream;
Let bells ding-dong and babies pong
Let the vicar baldly gleam:
Her 'I will' is consent, is semantic cement
And the rest of the day is a dream.

The reception affords one remarkable sight:
Somebody's cousin Morag
Trying to balance a plate and a glass,
Hold a toddler, gloves and handbag,
At the same time as clapping the best man's speech
And trying to light up a fag.

One glass of tepid sherry each
Is the caterer's regulations;
A lettuce leaf, some world-weary beef
And – because these are celebrations –
Some wafer-thin bread, frugally spread
With small, expired crustaceans.

But it's done at last. The speeches fade
Into decent obscurity;
The bride and groom nip off to her room
For a kiss and a cup of tea,
Then they dodge the mêlée by slipping away
In a commandeered MGB;

So they miss all the aerosols, tin cans, confetti,
The in-laws with saccharine menace;
The caparisoned car like a Turkish bazaar,
And the armpitty farewells from Dennis;
And, unfortunately, miss too the best man, who waits
With the tickets from Heathrow to Venice . . .

Everyone for Tennis

Unanswered questions lie about
Our universe like leaves:
Why Man? Why universe at all?
Why poverty, war, disease?
Who can enter the storehouse of the snow
Or bind the Pleiades?

Is Man an accidental blob
Of pure primaeval jelly?
How then Aquinas, Rembrandt, Newton,
Shakespeare, Botticelli?
And who gives a monkey's anyway –
There's tennis on the telly!

For it's summer, at last, and Wimbledon's here,
The fever is once more upon us;
We're in for a glut of self-image and strut
From white-shorted prima donnas.
No light-hearted quips from John McEnroe's lips
Just neanderthal bellows from Connors.

Ah! Wimbledon – home of strawberries and cream,
And of Dan Maskell's pre-main-verb-pauses;
Home of mild matrons and millionaires,
Lost matches, lost leaders, lost causes;
And girls with faces like Raphael angels
And calves like a battleship's hawsers.

It's almost, perhaps, appropriate,
In a world turned upside-down
That someone can win a zillion pounds,
Respect and world renown
For hitting a piece of rubber into
A box drawn on the ground.

And all across Britain babies will cry
And clamour in vain for a feed,
As mothers follow with bated breath
The fate of the number six seed
And whether he'll fall to a top-spun ball
From an unpronounceable Swede.

And husbands come home to Annabel Croft,
Leftovers, cheese and tined pears;
There's love-all been done, they've neglected his son,
There are glasses beneath all the chairs;
They've watched the whole lot of Willander-Mayotte –
They're engrossed, now, in Curran affairs.

'Net', 'First service', 'Forty-fifteen',
'Out' and 'New balls please';
The summer consists of sweat-banded wrists
And runic calls such as these,
And frills and lace on . . . every place,
And bronzed Hungarian knees.

And, of course, there's the usual dressing-room scene
When somebody rings from Hong Kong
Wanting a word with Jo Dury – 'Absurd!'
Says the steward, 'You can't: she's gone.'
'Gone where?' 'To play her first match of the day.'
'Oh, right,' says the voice, 'I'll hang on.'

But the poor old English language faces
The stiffest competition
From backhanders struck by Williams and Maskell
Who batter it into submission
As they slubber their mealy-mouthed platitudes
With quasi-erudition.

If you want to avoid Lendl, Becker and Lloyd,
If you're miffed by Mandlikova;
If the Wimbledon lawns reduce you to yawns
And you're sated with Schreiver and Stove;
Don't worry – it's only a fortnight, and then
It'll all be Navratil-over.

The W.I. and Mrs Dunn

For the seventieth anniversary of the National Federation of
Women's Institutes

Kissed by the golden light of the autumn sun
But kissed by no one else, stands Mrs Dunn.
She tidies a wisp of hair and says goodbye
At the Friday meeting of the W.I.
And smiles at Mrs Grey and Mrs Haynes,
And feels a cut below Miss Finchley-Staines;
Then trudges home beneath the darkening sky
To tea and toast and home-made apple pie.

Oh! Apple pie was what she made the best:
First prize at every fête – preserves came next,
Chutneys and country wines, sponge cakes and tarts;
The uncrowned village queen of homely arts.
None could knit as smooth, as fast as she –
A week for a jumper, and a month for three.
A teddy bear or giraffe with curious smirk
Adorned each Women's Institute sale of work.

She did it all, she said, because of Jack
(Framed on the mantelpiece in sober black)
And, when they left him in the churchyard, she
Transferred her love to jams and herbal tea
And filled the gap he'd left with busyness –
Thick winter scarves and mitts and woolly vests;
Mums don't have time, but she had time to spare
And filled it with love, new friends and pink mohair.

By every autumn half a hundred suns
Had shone on parsnip wine and perfect buns
Approved by the gentle smile of Ethel Haynes;
And then had come the young Miss Finchley-Staines.
Progressive, energetic, kindly too –
But knowing clearly what she had to do:
Remove the cobwebs, blow away the dust
From seventy years of worthy toil and rust.

And Mrs Dunn, alone with contrite tears,
Saw her whole life so many wasted years
Which should have been achieving social ends
In Church and Politics – not making friends
And cakes and clothes for babies. It was true:
Miss Finchley-Staines was clever, and she knew.
These skills were nothing but a source of pride
And Jack looked down at where she sat and cried.

Kissed by the dying rays of the autumn sun,
But kissed by no one else, sat Mrs Dunn.

Village Cricket
or
The Non-Player Trophy

The village green and two o'the clock;
A perfect day for sport,
Where, like a country proverb,
The scoreboard says 'nought for nought';
And A. G. MacDonell's shade shakes hands
With Hugh de Selincourt.

The hedges are choked with briar rose
Above the listless pools
Where dragonflies flash like veins of sun
And gnats model molecules,
And the umpire sucks his pipe and studies
The LBW rules.

This is just swank: he suffers from
Myopia, arthritis and gout,
And he's long since given up trying to be fair
Or tempering bias with doubt;
He works by the law of averages –
Every fifth appeal is 'out'.

The side consists of a postman, a printer,
An out-of-work jazz musician;
Two farmers, two teachers, a sales rep, a clerk
And an overweight obstetrician
Who's forged a Surrey sweater just
To frighten the opposition.

The pitch is thick with daisies and dock,
Toadstooled and pitted with holes;
It's laid on last season's football pitch –
Just in front of one of the goals.
The batsman's only real defence
Is by courtesy of the moles.

'Deep extra cover, Jim; Ray, at point',
Says the captain, a bit tongue in cheek;
He looked up the technical terms last night
And remembered them, too, by some freak;
But nobody knows what he's talking about
So they go where they went last week.

The village aged sit around
And draw lots for whose turn to recall
The day young Hubert clouted a six
Right over the churchyard wall;
And express their regret that this pansy set
Has no sense of tradition at all.

There's the one with the dreadful fear of the ball
Who stands on the boundary
And makes quite sure that the sun's in his eyes
And a catch will be hard to see;
He's worked out how to miss it by half an inch
And fall spectacularly.

The wicketkeeper smacks his gloves
In anticipatory glee;
Like Alan Knott, he moves a lot,
Waves arms and bends the knee;
And like the Ancient Mariner,
He stoppeth one of three.

The obstetrician's Lancia stands,
Its bodywork ticks in the sun;
It's the bodywork of its passenger that
Inspires the outfield to run.
She sits bored, sunglasses in her hair,
And listens to Radio 1.

Small children pester the batting side
As small horseflies pester stallions;
Linseed oil and new-mown grass
Bloom on the air. Batallions
Of Ian Botham look-unlikes
Strut round behind medallions.

Wives and girlfriends gossip and giggle
And clatter and clink and clup
As they chop and spread and slice and cut
And the sandwiches greyly pile up;
And they brew that deadly orange tea
That sets when it hits the cup.

It's during tea that the dog appears
From the depths of a shady thicket;
He pads across and sniffs the stumps
Then cocks his leg at the wicket,
No player and no gentleman,
But a connoisseur of cricket.

And They All Lived Happily Ever After . . .

It's an English State Occasion. Fire
The guns and ring the bells!
Someone we've never heard of's going
To marry someone else;
And London's going to look, all day,
Like a Pop-Up Book of Kells.

The pride, the pomp, the pageantry!
The pleasure it affords!
It's generally realized that
Some breastplates, plumes and swords
Can boost the ratings – sagging after
Wimbledon and Lords.

With a fervour unabated since
The first Elizabeth,
The nation – as a nation should –
Looks on and holds its breath;
But the BBC expels its wind
With a whiff of lexical death.

There's a special kind of language
Which the BBC employs
Called 'The Coronation Cliché', or,
By some, 'Blue Peter Voice':
Half an inch of meaning to
Each twenty feet of noise.

It's allusive, it's emetic and
It oozes out like oil;
It works like anaesthetic,
It's illiterately loyal:
Built on Bunyan, Buchan, Blyton,
Patience Strong and Conan Doyle.

It is noble and encrusted, it's
Ornate and periphrastic,
With blistering bouts of bathos,
Platitudinous, pleonastic;
With a mixture of mad metaphors
That's almost orgiastic.

If – heaven forbid! – there should occur
A hitch in the celebrations,
Some sycophant will treat us to
A few twee speculations
As to what the bride is thinking now;
But avoiding the word 'relations' . . .

And kind reporters, realizing
Our intolerable stress
At having to wait an hour or two
To see the wedding dress,
Will call in Judith Chalmers
Or Sue Cook to have a guess.

There'll be engineered embarrassment, too:
Roving microphones in full spate,
Extracting views and messages
From the inarticulate;
It's great (we hear), it's really great,
And the Princess? Well . . . she's great!

And families from Stoke-on-Trent
From Sidcup, Bognor, Beccles,
From Fishponds, Woking, Cockermouth,
From Exeter and Eccles,
Have come for their four-second glimpse
Of twenty-three blurred freckles.

And Mr and Mrs Average, who've
Been married for sixty years
Will give advice to the neophytes
Involving smiles and tears:
Scratch an English royalist
And Plato soon appears.

And when the final image fades
At the end of the long afternoon,
And England's a lump in the back of the throat,
Don't worry – you'll see them soon:
They've sent Desmond Wilcox along in the coach
To film the honeymoon.

Insufferable, The Little Children

1. Why art thou so vexed, O my soul: and why art thou so disquieted within me?
2. Thou must be joking when thou sayest they are breaking up already: I mean, we have scarcely got through the Easter eggs.
3. O, what sins have I committed: that I am chastened as with a rod?
4. After six weeks of uninterrupted Wayne and Tracy: wormwood and gall will be as nectar and ambrosia.
5. Whither shall I go for peace and quiet: or where shall I hide me from their clamour?
6. If I climb the stairs they are there: if I go down, even to the living-room, they are there also.
7. My days are gone like a shadow: and I am withered like grass.
8. Their iniquities are more in number than the sand: so also are their sullen little friends with bellicose temperaments, too much pocket-money, hollow legs, unquenchable thirsts, fog-horn voices, dripping noses and mercilessly tardy bedtimes.
9. Wayne doth send out his voice, yea, and that a mighty voice: remove him from my sight lest I smite him upon the hip.
10. Who maketh the windows to shake: and his bedroom as a battlefield.
11. He pulleth the hair of his sister's head, and knappeth her dolls in sunder: she therefore hath put sawdust in his Branflakes.
12. Six is it of one: yea, and half a dozen of the other.
13. Daily they say unto me: 'Mummy, what can I do next?'
14. Unto whom I sware in my wrath: and instantly regretted it.

15. They lay waste the kitchen like a whirlwind: storm and tempest fulfilling their words.
16. O, how amiable were my dwellings: and just look at them now.
17. By the washing-machine I sat down and wept: by the fridge-freezer I uttered my reproof.
18. One day in July or August: feels something like a thousand. *Amen*

Second-Class Citizens

If we're all unique, all different –
And some say the fact is plain –
Can anyone tell me why it is
That, whenever you get on a train,
You meet the same predictable types
Over and over again?

It could just be coincidence,
But I can't believe it, so
I'm working on a theory that
Some British Rail P.R.O.
Actually hires these archetypes
To maintain the status quo.

You've all seen the sort I'm talking about:
The Scotsman, unconscious at last,
Surrounded by empty McEwans cans;
The frail lady – ex-first-class –
Who nods at the green good manners
Of the English fields that pass.

There's the beauty who sits by the window and reads
But who never will catch your eye;
The man who fidgets and will unloose
Banalities, by and by;
And the lady who's checked with *every*one, twice,
That this train *will* stop at Rye.

There's the business man: two types are found –
The one with inch-thick piles
Of photostats and export bills
Who scribbles and ticks and files;
And the one who's asleep as he hits the seat
And snores for the next eighty miles.

There's the eater who's trying terribly hard
To eat without making a mess;
To masticate politely – you
Can see he's in distress
And the eyes of the carriage are all upon
His vast French sandwich . . . with cress . . .

There's always an elderly couple, arm
In arm, across the aisle;
He provides the compulsory struck-match smell,
She is silent for mile after mile;
He smokes a pipe, has a rolled plastic mac,
A thermos and a smile.

There's the impresser, usually a man,
Pretending to read Solzhenitsyn
Or something else intellectual
With Greek and Latin bits in;
But the cover, you'll note, is very wide
So that Asterix just fits in.

There's the child, all curls and plastic pants
Who, tired of counting her toes
And colouring purple cows and sheep,
Turns her mother a rich shade of rose
By pointing out to the carriage at large:
'That man's got a pimply nose!'

There's the mental dwarf with the personal stereo
Used most *im*personally,
Which fills the air with the mad despair
Of a trapped, soprano bee;
A kind of prolonged but effective do-it–
Yourself lobotomy.

There's the crossword doer who fills in *The Times*
In five and a half minutes flat;
When he goes to the loo he leaves it behind
And when you look under his hat,
He's filled it with Zixcov and Qwerdlip and Sproo,
And clever words like that.

And which type are you? I'd hazard a guess
The cool beauty will get the most votes;
Are you sure you don't recognize yourself
In the other sheep or goats?
Me? Oh, I'm the one with the little brown book
Furtively making notes.

Sea Fret

I must down to the seas again,
To the lonely sea and the sky,
Where half a million shoulderblades
Are oiled and ready to fry;
And bodies that winter has gratefully veiled
Come out and appal the eye;

And father is bluff and hearty and scoffs:
'Just a crab! Pick it up! Be a man!'
And he picks it up with a chuckle of scorn
And loses the use of one hand;
And grandmother ponders the memories brought
By a gusset full of sand;

And the local youths have constructed a goal
Out of jackets and cans of beer;
'To me! Barry! To me! To me!
Barry! To me! Over here!'
And the girls, unimpressed go on building a nest
Of crash-helmets and Ambre-Solaire;

While the wholemeal parents have taken Cassandra
For an ecological spin
To the farming museum, the butterfly park
And the oak that cloaked a King,
When all she wants is a bucket and spade
And a friend with a cockney grin;

And Kevin, by accident, brushes the hand
Of his next-door neighbour's daughter
Who watches the tide receding as fast
As the things that her mother has taught her,
And the darkling beach spins a long double line
Of footprints filling with water;

And the boarding-house smell (of wet plimsolls and gas
And polish) pervades the gloom
Where father watches the Test highlights
In the bare little TV room;
And mother is hopeful in underwear
Like she wore on her honeymoon;

And when it's all over, the luggage is lugged,
And everyone's tired and snappy,
For they got up to pack at a quarter past five
And the baby's just filled his fourth nappy;
Was it worth all the bother? For only the dog
Has been *truly* and *blissfully* happy.

A Sound Education

William Makepeace Morris was
An extraordinary boy,
Who from his birth refused and scorned
Each Teddy, book and toy,

And every moment of the day
Throughout his childhood years
He'd employ in imitating all
That fell upon his ears.

At seven months, a tweet-tweet-tweet
From moss'd cottage apple-boughs
Evoked a tweet-tweet-tweet from Bill;
He could do the same with cows.

A horse might neigh in a field close by,
Then neighs would cascade from Bill;
It's not suprising the doctor thought
Him terminally ill.

At eighteen months – with the radio and
Each visitor as his research-field –
His vocabularly quite outstripped
That of Levin or Burgess or Burchfield.

The words to him were meaningless,
He just spoke them with precision;
His parents rightly thought he'd make
An excellent politician.

But sounds were what he loved the best
A distant, barking dog,
Or the wistful whine of a mouth-organ
That echoed in the fog.

By the age of twelve he'd a repertoire
That lasted sixty hours
Including tapirs mating
In a bed of cauliflowers,

And underground trains and bubbling drains
And submarines and sirens,
And other noises guaranteed
To empty the environs.

At school he did the noises off
For the Drama Society:
They still recall the Henry V
Of nineteen sixty-three –

The *snarl* he gave when they reached the line
'Then imitate the action
Of the tiger' left the head
A month and a half in traction.

But, leaving school, he was always a squarish
Peg in a roundish hole;
He tried accountancy, gardening, welding,
And finished up on the dole.

And then there was a major fire
In the BBC sound-effect archives;
And William Makepeace Morris walked
Straight in, and saved their lives.

In eighteen months he'd re-recorded
The sounds of fifty years;
He'd earned himself a fortune
But he left the place in tears;

There was one effect he couldn't get
Though he tried and tried again;
They wanted the sound of sixty thousand
Drunken laundrymen

At a cricket match during a bombing raid
On a zoo, by an organ-tuner
While the massed bands of the Coldstream guards
Passed by on a full-rigged schooner.

At the four-hundredth take he threw in the towel:
The replay confirmed his fears –
He'd got it all perfect except for the Coldstreams.

He'd done the Grenadiers.

Culture and Anarchy

Has anyone ever, I wonder, been able
To find something really inviting
To do when you're out and you're at a loose end
And a vicious north-easterly's biting
So hard that the litter's six feet off the ground –
Which the pigeons find somewhat exciting.

And the rain's hissing down from the sky's purple frown
And the afternoon light's growing thick;
'Museums!' you think, 'Country Houses – that's right,
Art galleries; which shall I pick?'
And you clutch at this classy and cultural scheme
As a drowning man clutches a brick.

You see, half the galleries pullulate
With thin beards in search of catharses;
Exhibitions of ethno-eccentric dismay
Which appeal to the mueslied classes,
Such as 'Psycho-Accidental Art'
Or 'Latvian Moose-Harness Brasses'.

And the country house has a sanctified smell
Like long Sunday afternoons;
Acres of polish, untouchable urns,
Glass cases of china and spoons;
The woodcarving may be by Gibbons, but then
The pictures are all by baboons.

The Royal Academy proudly boasts,
Through hundreds of small despairs,
The usual post-Hockney, post-Bacon and such,
Some feminist underarm hairs,
Geraniums, fairgrounds, abstracts, and several
Nondescript ladies on chairs.

Museums – or is it musea? – burn
With a cold, intellectual flame;
You feel you ought to be fired, but then
You can't – and, oh! the shame!
And Madame Tussaud's, since Spitting Image,
Will never be quite the same.

So, where do you go at a time like this?
To the National Gallery
Where everyone's favourite painting, somehow,
Always seems to be.
You can drink your fill at the wells of Art –
And get a cup of tea.

But what's this in room ten? Something
Juvenile this way comes;
A refugee from the 'William' books
With half a dozen chums,
Rushing from Rubens to Veronese
Counting all the bums.

The teacher was hoping to miss out this room,
But Bronzino's attracted the tour:
'Miss, who is the lady without any clothes?
And what are they squeezing her for?'
And, later, of Holbein's 'Ambassadors' –
'Look, one of them's sicked on the floor!'

And there rises a scent, from the Umbrian school
At odds with those mystical scenes:
Something a cross between old non-drip gloss
And overcooked haricot beans –
The primitive, punitive, primary-school smell
Of warm socks and wet gaberdines.

But the children have done what a critic won't dare;
They've no preconceptions in store.
The questions that naturally rise to their lips
Are ones that you can't ignore:
Who *is* that lady without any clothes?
And what *are* they squeezing her for?

Come on! Let's be honest – culture's OK
If you're working to get a degree,
But nothing can measure the exquisite pleasure
Of a sofa, a cat on your knee,
A packet of crisps and a bottle of beer
And a Test-match to watch on TV.

Only Collect

Collecting's not a hobby; it's
An unassuageable passion
Dedicated to the premise:
Taste Is Merely Fashion.
Now England's a nation of grot-keepers
And everyone wants his ration.

It can turn life's richest counterpoint
To a monothematic drone;
It can cabin, crib, confine, cut off
(A collector is always alone)
For the end is not just to find the best
But to have it as your own.

Now collections can be of anything
That's ever existed on earth;
But a dedicated collector
Is someone who's learned from birth
That only the ephemeral
Is of really lasting worth.

It isn't at all a spectator sport,
But merely a way to use
The endemic, covetous instinct
Of those who have IQs
Only a little larger than
The size they take in shoes.

You can bore your way through parties like
The proverbial butter-knife;
You can qualify for a MenCap grant
You can alienate your wife
By turning serendipity
Into a way of life.

When a like becomes a want becomes
A need becomes a must,
You know your collecting instinct is
Just one step down from lust;
And you're classed as a real collector
When your collection's collecting dust.

Oh, we may have imperilled our wildlife
And perhaps we'll destroy the sea,
But we'll never run out, now, of biscuit-tins
Made in nineteen twenty-three,
Or spinning-tops or old bus-stops
Or honeypots shaped like a bee.

Bakelite fingernail-buffers, inkwells,
Toby-jugs, thimbles and steins;
Tibetan hand-carved bidet covers,
Rail tickets from long-disused lines;
A freshen-up tissue from each airline's issue,
Whole albums of doorbell designs.

Surgical instruments, beer-bottle tops,
You can make any field your own;
For the only important thing about
A collection is how it has grown;
Quality's sometimes a factor, or course,
But extent is a sine qua non.

And once you've decided on what you'll collect,
However inane it appears,
You're bound to become an authority
If you do it for two or three years.
It's cute, it's loot, and a good substitute
For having creative ideas.

For the narrower your subject is,
The more quickly your knowledge increases
Till you know just a part of a part of a part
Of one of life's tiniest pieces.
It's a craft the universities teach,
Only there it's called 'writing a thesis'.

Just think! When you next go to dinner with friends
And you're handed a large G and T,
Some bright so-and-so says 'Whaddya know?'
You can offer the company:
'There are one thousand two hundred and four semi-colons
In *Under the Greenwood Tree*.'

'Tis a Mad World, My Masters

England is full of maniacs
From Berwick-on-Tweed to Cheam;
Crusaders, men with a single idea,
Fanatics with a dream;
Hair awry and a maddened eye
Like a kind of visual scream.
The madness takes a thousand forms
But a proselytizing strain
Characterizes every one
And often supplants the brain
Which, if they've got one at all, moves as fast
As a cake left out in the rain;
It hasn't decayed, but it's been delayed
During some childhood fervour;
It's as if they got stuck at nine years old
And can't get any further.
Like the man who joins the Sealed Knot
For a personal kind of catharsis
And re-enacts Sedgemoor and Stamford Bridge
As ragged, historical farces,
Self-conscious in ill-fitting clothes
And *always* with watch and glasses.
There's the one who turns his Barratt Home
To a replica of Crewe,
All points and sidings and papier-mâché
And balsa-wood and glue;
He'll frighten you with the Brighton Belle
As you step inside the loo.
There are national fanatics as well, of course,
Like David Bellamy
Up to his crutch in mud and such
And covered in badger's pee,

And Patrick Moore's head like an unmade bed
Speaking at mach 3.
But there's one makes them all look tame,
One who's Camembert to their Brie,
And that's the electro-techno-quadro-
Audio devotee
And his micro-laser graphic modal
TSCO3
With variable input-synchro
Wave-state parity
To equalize the filter decay
With sound-opacity
Combined with two-way ratio-hold
On high-bias density,
And thus make balanced speaker-function
On a DX 623
When using amp. defeat reduction-
Output on CD.
So you can't play 'Für Elise' now
Without a BSc.
What started off as audio
Is now theology;
And simple music-lovers can be
Burned for heresy.

Five minutes with a Hi-Fi freak
And I lose my compos mentis
And start to pray for a quick replay
Of 'The Sorcerer's Apprentice',
Where all the techno marvels go
Berserk and start to crumble,
And mangled tapes, in serpent shapes,
Crawl through the woofers' rumble;
Lights flash wildly, filters fizz
Hot metal starts to dribble –
It's called 'Carl Nielsen's Last Revenge'

For it's Inextinguishable.
No, if you're looking for the best
In High–Fidelity,
Forget your Nad, your Yamaha,
Forget your JVC,
The highest faith of all is found
In English poetry.

Laetatus Prom

1. I was glad when they said unto me: we will go into the Albert Hall.
2. For, lo, the summer is come: and this is the nth season of Henry Wood Promenade Concerts.
3. Our feet shall freeze to the stones of Prince Consort Rd.: he that sitteth there shall not sleep.
4. Behold, he that keepeth thy place: had jolly well better not slumber nor sleep.
5. They shall come from the south and from the west: even they that dwell in the uttermost parts of Surrey.
6. I had rather be a doorkeeper in the Albert Hall: than dwell in a sleeping-bag in the queue.
7. There shall be a new hero for the promenaders: and it shall almost certainly be he that conducteth 'The Rite of Spring'.
8. Who stilleth the raging of 'La Mer' and somehow getteth through the 'Turangalila' Symphony.
9. Richard Baker will be there: yea, announcements shall be on his lips and he shall speak forth with joy.
10. Which is not surprising when you think about it: the best seat in the house and that entirely free.
11. Brahms shall we hear, and much great Mozart: Mahler also shall be from everlasting to everlasting.
12. O clap your hands all ye peoples: but remember to do so before the last movement has finished.
13. Lo, whenever a piano is played: and the lid thereof is lifted
14. 'Heave' shall they shout, and yet another night shall they shout 'Heave': and it shall be for a mighty joke.
15. Those in the front row shall be spotty, overweight and of gloomy countenance: one shall follow the score, and one shall nod in time. Almost.

16. The multitude shall hold up banners and soft toys: to prove they take things seriously.
17. Webern shall be played by foreign ensembles: Xenakis also and Penderecki, Berio, Skalkottas and Lutoslawski.
18. They will not lift up their eyes unto the conductor: from whence cometh no help.

    Glory be to Skriabin: and to Bruckner, and to Havergal Brian.

    As it was in 1890, is now and ever shall be: works without end, *Amen*.

Wish You Were Here

Oh, an English beach on a summer's day
Is a glorious place to be;
Where lovers lie glued – and practically nude –
And grandfathers chain-drink tea,
And maiden ladies surrender themselves
To the rough, male kiss of the sea.

And flies won't land on the hearth-hot sand
But on ankles and buttocks and hips;
And golden lads pant for bikini'd girls
Like greyhounds in the slips;
There's the smell of diesel, doughnuts, dogs
And distant fish and chips.

There are seaweed smells and ice-cream bells
And a hullabaloo of balloons;
And a sweating band on the brave grandstand,
Pumping out brassy tunes;
And the gulls create like nails on a slate
Through the long, blue afternoons.

There are Venuses and Adonises
Like a seven-stone weakling's dream:
And children by the champagne sea
With wince and whinny and scream;
And massive mothers like pale blancmange
Topped off with sun-tan cream.

There's the lonely boy with the cowed half-smile,
And limbs like a small clothes-prop;
He waits on the fringe of the cricket match
As a volunteer long-stop,
But he's never asked to bat or bowl,
Or share a bottle of pop.

And the soaking dog that shakes itself
Over the egg mayonnaise;
And father says, 'You naughty dog!'
At least – in paraphrase;
And the dog flops down behind its tongue
With a Saint Sebastian gaze.

And the sandwiches are flattened and damp
And slightly more sand than wich;
And Dad's very proud of the castle he's built –
A bit like a forties fridge;
While the Volvo driver next door is constructing
The Sydney Harbour Bridge.

He's got the lot: the windbreak, the groundsheet,
The folding table and chair,
Beach-barbecue, lilos, check serviettes,
2·4 kids who don't swear,
A surfboard that looks like a portable Porsche
And a pigeon chest matted with hair.

So it's nice when his camp has to break up and flee
From the incoming tide's advance;
And demonstrate to the general delight
The great British Blanket Dance
With a scattering of underwear, watches and spades
And a flurry of fragile aunts.

If you've ever seen husband, wife, pekinese,
As like as three peas in a pod,
Or the square-jawed, blond-haired suntanned type
Auditioning for a god,
Or old men's necks as red as plums
And their legs as white as cod;

If you've ever watched anyone trying to get dressed
Without breaking the decency laws;
Or mountains of She at the edge of the sea
With their dresses pulled up to their drawers,
You'll realize that Donald McGill and I
Don't do caricatures.

Home Thoughts from the Broads

I must home from the sea again,
But shouldn't have gone today:
The M's 1, 2, 3, 4, 5, 6
Are subject to delay;
And we broke down once outside Skegness
And twice in Harringay.

And arriving back with a dripping sump
And a smell of burning oil,
The car gave a last, spasmodic twitch
And shuffled off its coil;
And the house was a tomb in which every room
Was like something from Conan Doyle.

For the light switch clicks in a dead sort of way:
The electrics have gone kaput,
Which explains why Dad ends up on the floor
With a mouthful of Mum's left foot
And something else (later explained as a portion
Of quite a large fall of soot).

And the damp has come up in the dining-room
Like a dog through a paper hoop,
And the Aga's making funeral sounds
Like a granite slab with croup,
And the sink's half full of something like
Senescent oxtail soup;

And the table is littered with buff envelopes
With windows – all lettered in red,
And the spiders upstairs have had torrid affairs
And left children all over the bed,
And everyone thought someone else had bought
The bacon, the eggs and the bread.

And the tap on the bath that was dripping a bit
Has increased to a steadyish stream
And invested the walls of the rooms downstairs
With a sub-Atlantic gleam,
And father denies that he left the plug in
And enlarges on his theme.

And the fridge has committed suicide
Its insides are all green and hairy
And the cat was locked in for a day or two
And set traps for all the unwary
And performed the ultimate critical act
On the overfed canary.

But a nice cup of tea and a spot of TV
And a word with the garden gnome –
Well, the holiday's done and it wasn't much fun
In the sting of the wind and the foam;
A rose to be sure is a rose is a rose,
But a home is a home is a home.

MIDWEEKENDINGS

Before the Show

A Green-room, at the best of times,
Is a strange sort of place to be:
It has a perplexing, no-man's-landish
Ambiguity.
Especially at eight thirty-two
In the bowels of the BBC,

Where people from all walks of life
Rub shoulders (sometimes more)
And stare with self-defensive gaze
At the slowly opening door
To see if it's someone they ought to impress
Or with whom they can wipe the floor.

You've seen dogs meeting in the street
And what they . . . like to do;
This is the human equivalent –
Sycophancy's as potent as glue –
And each *famous* guest increases the flow
By ten to the power two.

There's a lot of superficial laughter
And loudish bonhomie
Despite the absence of anything stronger
Than orange, coffee or tea –
At least, until they get permission
To raise the licence fee.

The unlikeliest people strike sparks at once:
Politicians and models, of course,
While writers eye one another up
As a gypsy eyes a horse,
And the inexperienced tap their feet
In a kind of nervous morse.

A female guest provokes a kind
Of shuffle among the males,
So that half stand up and cough, half sit –
Uncertain what custom prevails
For she might be a feminist come in disguise
With painted fingernails.

There's always a guilty, breathless hush
When a clergyman enters the room;
A kindly light but an awful blight
Which creates the encircling gloom;
This is Live Radio! . . . Almost as live
As Amen-Hotep's tomb.

The old hands sit and say nothing at all,
So the chairman is falsely bright;
The smell of fear is strong and clear
And nothing is going right;
And the producer debates the ethics of
Getting a Bishop tight.

Or opera singers gargle and shriek
At their vocal exercises;
Or an MP might say something honest
(The Green-room is full of surprises);
Or the controller of Radio 4 might come in
To observe some major crises

Like the birthday guest not appearing at all,
He could be in Knightsbridge or Alnwick,
The staff are on five phones at once –
Though all that they do in their panic
Is tantamount to re-arranging
The deckchairs on the *Titanic*.

But somehow the show gets done. Somehow
We get the producer's OK.
(That's a rough translation of 'Wonderful, darlings!
Super, loves! What can I say?!')
And we try not to think it'll happen again
Next week, in just the same way.

Portrait Gallery

Roger McGough Roger McGough as a guest on Midweek?
Isn't one poet more than enough?
So, what can I say about his verse?
Except: 'I like that stuff'!
It combines the diurnal grind and grit
With surreal logic-chopping
And comes out as a cross between Auden and Donne
And a nice fresh parrot-dropping.

Michael Palin Welcome to Michael Palin – a fellow
Of wit and erudition,
Who attends these Private Functions in
His Missionary Position.

Anthony Burgess Anthony Burgess's learning
And Klangfarbenmelodie
Can stretch from St Paul to Napoleon via
Steatopygous Enderby.
But have you heard Burgess's music?
Or Bruckner's poetry?
They're going to be done at the Proms this year
With the Shakespeare Mass in C.
Farewell writers, actors, singers,
Purveyors of interviews;
And which will be left in the memory when
The End of the World *isn't* News?

Richard Gordon

They tell me the first book was not a success,
The critics were grudging and rude,
Until Richard Gordon took out a colon
And had the appendix removed.
I'm surrounded by medics – Garden and Gordon
And Salter (all Doctors on Toast);
You don't want a Forde as your poet today,
But a Housman might well fill the post . . .

Ivor Cutler

It's quite hard to class Ivor Cutler;
He's an architect of the absurd,
A suavely surrealist songster,
A dour Scots Magritte of the Word.

Tom Conti

I hope we've made you feel at home
('Glittering Prizes' all over again)
Having sparkling conversation
Round a bottle of champagne.
I can see you're trying to stifle a yawn.
That's the trouble with instant Forde;
My poems have a kind of veneer,
But they end up as Conti bored.

John Wells

It's libel when it's written down,
It's slander when it's said;
But when it's on the stage, and works,
It's called John Wells instead.

He's shown us all this morning
(If we needed to be shown)
The febrile, fatuous fuddled face
Of the power behind the crone.

85

His Dennis Thatcher's gained a place
In half the world's affections
Explaining, at the same time, why
The Don't-Knows win the elections.

Champagne today for Ernie Wise,
Though his birthday came and went;
This is what is called, I suppose,
'Wise after the event' . . .
It's a privilege to drink to one
Who's managed to evince
More belly-laughs per second squared
Than any before or since.
When it comes to classics, Rome had Virgil
The Dutch had Rembrandt; Iti's
Can boast of Vivaldi; the Germans had Bach,
But we had Morecambe and Wise.

Champagne for Mr Atkinson
And as it trickles down
Let's drink a health to the man with the pan-
Melancholicocilious frown.
There aren't that many comedians
Whom, when off-screen, people miss;
And ever fewer who are talked of in terms
Of their Zob and their Orifice.

I've worked backwards through the O.E.D.
From Zygospore to Bangkok,
And I still can't find a decent rhyme
To go with Kenneth Williams.
Kenneth Williams – erudite,
Witty, with all the graces;
And a tongue that can maim at a hundred yards
And kill at fifty paces.

Mgr Bruce Kent	Mgr Bruce Kent, our birthday guest, Has taken a lot of stick For daring to think his beliefs might have A bearing on politics.
	The Church has often been criticized For refusing a difficult choice; For sitting on moral fences And lowering its voice;
	Then, when its leaders *do* speak out, The politicians jeer That if the Church has accents at all, They shouldn't be loud or clear.
Peter de Savery	Let foundations discuss, debate, Sponsorship or not; Peter has caused a semantic change: It's now called 'sponsoryacht' . . .
John Hillaby	England, Europe, Africa – All in a year's excursion; Another William Cobbett, but The international version.
	John Hillaby's the kind of man Who admits of no restriction. He probably reads Hammond Innes as well – And thinks it's all non-fiction.
Jonathan Dimbleby	I suppose both he and David have set Themselves up as prime knockables In that they've dared to follow in A distinguished father's vocables.

Tam Dalyell

We may have found that uncommon thing,
An honest politician –
As rare as a librarian's smile
Or a teetotal musician.

So, a welcome to our birthday guest,
The MP Tam Dalyell:
You may not have heard the Tam D bit
But you must have heard the yell!

And the MP bit's confusing, too;
To me it means 'mezzo piano'
Which is not a fair description of
His stance on the *Belgrano* . . .

Colonel Blashford-Snell

Colonel Blashford-Snell I've found
Quieter and modester
Than the cross I expected between Columbus,
Dan Dare and C. S. Forester.

He's certainly a kind of twentieth-
Century Marco Polo:
If no one else will risk their necks
He'll go and do it solo.

Group Captain Peter Townsend

He could teach us actors, poets,
Painters, a thing or two;
For what he's *still* most famous for
Is something he didn't do.

It's nothing like a fairy-tale
And everything like success
To live happily ever after by
Not marrying a Princess . . .

Jack Ashley MP

The disadvantaged have Jack to thank
For many a motion tabled.
On their behalf he raises Cain –
The first one to be dis-Abeled . . .

His deep and genuine concern
Is due to what he's been through;
Perhaps all MPs should be more au fait
With the causes they mean to pursue.

Thus, the Minister for the Arts would find
Each year that his income would fall,
And the Minister for Employment wouldn't
Have a job at all.

The Minister for Sport would carry
Aerosols, bike-chains, ploughshares.
One can only dream of the training scheme
For the Ministry of Foreign Affair(e)s . . .

Mike Leigh

Actors have found a new way to think:
The Keith-and-Candice-Marie-Way.
That's what happens when you give
Your cast a touch of Leighway.

It's hard to define Mike Leigh's work,
Its varieties of darkness:
A sort of 'Revenge' Alan Ayckbourn,
Without his proscenium archness.

Alan Ayckbourn

Mind you – he's not just laughs: he sees
The skull beneath the skin.
While he's tickling you under the armpits
He bashes you on the shin.

All he needs is an empty space,
Three ducks and a divan;
The bard of the Barrat houses.
Congreve – in Acrilan.

Robert Maxwell

The light of the sun when he deigns to unfold it
Depends on the organ that tries to behold it.
Of course British papers are not all the same;
What you get from your daily depends on your aim –
You go to the *Guardian* for misprints galore,
There are boobs in the *Mirror* – well, not any more:
They've been covered up with wet T-shirts and lace
So the reader (of course) only looks at the face.
Now the physicists tell me, a mirror takes light
And reverses the truth, so that left turns to right,
But astronomers say, without hint of a pun,
It's the very best way to look at the sun.
Can someone explain? It would be a great kindness –
Does it *really* reflect? Or induce total blindness?

Desmond Morris

There's certainly been a lack of needless
Movement among those assembled;
No drummings or twitchings or chewings of nails
Or hostilities quietly dissembled.

But Desmond Morris is used to that,
You can see by the look in his eyes;
This lack of disguising just covers up
The disguises we try to disguise.

Gerald Scarfe

From Peer or Bishop, 'tis no easy thing
To draw the man who *loves* his God or King;
But if you'd see instead the other half,
Entreat th' envenomed pen of Gerald Scarfe.
The exactest traits of body or of mind
We owe to Scarfe and others of his kind
Who fasten savagely upon some flaw –
A wart, a pointed nose, a sagging jaw –
And, by a kind of visual metonomy,
Can criticize a nation's whole economy.

Roy Hudd

He's got a thousand miles of jokes,
He's got gags by the gallon,
But he's best pleased doing sweet F.A. –
That's Flanagan and Allen.

Mind you, Roy can be difficult,
No shadow of a doubt:
They say there's nothing he can't make
A song and dance about.

Michael Grade
Controller BBC 1

He's a birthday guest, and those who are thinking
Of getting out the meat-axe –
Calm yourselves! Go and watch
The Pick of This Year's Ceefax.

'Controller' is a surprising term;
The control *may* be tremendous,
But it still lets through 'The Dukes of Hazzard'
'That's Life' and 'Eastenders'!

91

She

Those who know my poems well
Will know the lavish praise
I heap upon those dullnesses
Thrust into public gaze
Who cast shadows on all our tomorrows
And darken our yesterdays.

The Rantzens, the Hartys, the Russell Grants –
I've no need to prolong the list: it
's true, you can watch a whole programme of theirs
And still believe you've missed it.

There's all the hosts of game shows
And the razzamatazz they've brought us;
Egophiles with razored smiles
Like a constipated tortoise.

There's Terry Wogan – the reason he talks
Such infinite reams of rot is
He's still got bits of Blarney stone
Hung round his epiglottis.

Then there's politicians; let's be fair,
Beneath that glib exterior
Scratch down a bit and you'll find that there's
Another glib exterior.

But there's an unsung TV star,
Not a 'personality'
But just as well known as Wogan
And on more frequently;

An enigmatic creature,
A dove, a doe, a pearl;
The best-known figure on the box –
The BBC test-card girl.

Each day she performs her selfless task
With tireless devotion,
Professional to the fingertips,
Sans motive, script or motion.

From the director's call for 'action'
To, twelve hours later, 'cut!'
She doesn't move a muscle;
It's a feat of endurance, but

I long to know, and dare not ask
This media colossus
Why can't she finish off a simple
Game of noughts and crosses?

What's she called? Is she Sharon, Tracey, Shirl?
Or, knowing the BBC,
Is she Charlotte or Cassandra
Or a little Antiope?

If I knew her name I'd write to her
And tell her to beware,
For the Winston Churchill Obscenity Act
Will get that teddy-bear!

She's certainly predictable,
But that should not offend us:
It's a quality we seem to like
In sit-coms or 'EastEnders'.

She ages very slowly
'Cos she doesn't move a lot;
But she's bound to grow up one day
And be a . . . well – *be what?*

She'd make a great Hermione
In *The Winter's Tale* one of these days;
A Post-Office assistant,
A stuntman for 'Songs of Praise'.

So here's a little quiz for you;
What sort of job can you find
For one who's never had to work
Or even use her mind?

Someone stuck in the distant past
Unwilling to move or speak?
Answers on a postcard, please,
And send them to 'Midweek'.

Sonnets CLI and CLII

To the onlie begetter, Miss Kate Moon,
continuity announcer, by Mr. W.S.

CLI

No form hast thou, save that mine eye has made;
These gentle vocables thy substance are.
Reith shall not boast thou walkest in his shade:
He is eclipsed – thou art the morning star.
Let dullards hearken to the works of Liszt,
To 'Any Answers', 'Checkpoint' or 'Today';
It is that voice between that I have missed,
And do miss still, and long to hear it say
'We have some time in hand before our talk
On "Kant, the Novel and the Welfare State"',
Or, as the bacon dangles from my fork,
'The time is almost twenty-five past eight'.
Such is my love, so would I do thee service,
I'll even stay tuned in through Libby Purves.

CLII

And when the last page of *Radio Times* is turned;
When aging couples yawn and douse the light;
When my poor candle at both ends has burned
From 'Six a.m.' through to 'The World Tonight',
I know you smile because you must pretend
To give to all men what is mine by right –
Your final words: 'That brings us to the end
Of broadcasting on Radio 4 tonight.'
Mine eye doth play the painter and I see
Thy beauty's form descend the darkling stairs
Down to reception where Security
Gives a half-smile, but knows you not, nor cares.
Click, click; your heels across the marble floor.
A pause. A whiff of night. A swinging door.

Part 2:
XENOPHOBIA–ZOIC

Here's Egg on your Face

To distinguish Man from the animals
Takes some intellectual bottle;
It's been tried by Kant, Bronowski, Ayer,
Plato and Aristotle:
If not every theory depends on them,
Certainly quite a lot'll.

Monogamy, a skill with tools,
An exclusive upright grace
Have all been cited as foolproof ways
To define the human race;
A simpler way would be to say
Man can have egg on his face.

Just watch the man who's got to buy 'Things'
From the Feminine Hygiene section,
Or any writer from Mills and Boon
At a literary reception;
Or look at Mrs Thatcher's face
After the next by-election.

Or a scriptwriter for 'Little and Large'
(Just to stretch your imagination)
Coming up with a witty line
And blowing his reputation.
Embarrassments all, but there is a much more
Awkward situation.

You're walking down a corridor, and
An acquaintance hoves in view;
You've nothing to say, but you must be polite,
So what are you going to do?
Give a smile, or a nod, or perhaps a murmured
'Morning!' or 'How are you?'

But on the way back, he's there again;
Just him, no one else, so, once more
Some sort of greeting, of course, is required –
And not quite the same as before;
Well, only a fool would be lost for words,
So you open your mouth and 'Horhor!'

You purse your lips and raise your brows
Or do your Eccles 'Har-low!'
Or put on a cod Al Jolson smile
Just to show that you're fun to know
And self-consciousness is as far away
As the nearest Eskimo.

Your eyes protrude, you waggle your head,
You embarrass your*self* with shame;
The only consolation is
That *he* does precisely the same;
You feel a fool, but what can you do?
There's no rules for this sort of game.

Back in the office you sit for a while
Feeling strangely disturbed and upset;
There ought to be a code laid down
For meeting a man you've just met;
A stock of witty remarks you could make
That no one could ever forget.

But whatever you think of's a bit too much –
A little too consciously 'clever';
Could you use some props? Plastic doggy-drops?
A puppet? Or could you endeavour
Always to leave the room in a disguise
So the problem would vanish for ever?

Well, the incident fades (as incidents do);
Only . . . when you go off for a tea,
And close the door behind you,
Down the corridor you see
A single figure approaching again –
And you know who it's going to be . . .

There's nothing you can do this time,
Short of metamorphosis;
Or the arch, ill-chosen, flaccid phrase:
'We can't go on meeting like this!'
Or pretend a sudden interest in
The carpet's psoriasis.

You can see the awful moment coming
A minute or more away;
The smiles switch on, the brain has gone,
Idiocy rules, OK.
'My wife's beginning . . .' 'Do you always come . . .'
'To suspect!', 'the pretty way?' . . .

There is a way to get out of it:
Turn it into a game –
You quote a line of poetry
And he's got to do the same;
Then, if you subsequently meet,
You guess the author's name.

This way you learn some poetry,
(Which can't be bad, at least),
All fear of walking corridors
Will very soon have ceased,
And a visit to the loo becomes
A literary feast.

It's no use Looking for an Editorial in a Tablecloth Simply Because you Eat your Meals off a Newspaper

A nail in the coffin of cliché-mongers
Who're getting too big for their boots;
They give the language a very bad press
And what *don't* they give? Two hoots.

The exponents of cliché do damage – (what sort?
'Untold') both to thought and their souls;
They can't just 'not touch' they have to employ
Incontiguous barge-poles.

Test yourself on the following questions:
One mark for each you knew –
With a score of something less than one
You may possibly have an I.Q.

How do rumours spread? Like wildfire.
Are injuries had? No, 'sustained';
After pandemonium had broken loose
What did Peace do? 'Reigned'.

With what small thing do you show esteem?
The answer is 'a token';
And beams may be termed simply 'oak', but chests
Are invariably 'oaken'.

Ignorance is always 'blissful',
Cheek is 'brazen', a lie
Is 'barefaced'; what word always goes with impossible?
Only one – 'well-nigh'.

And let the emptor caveat:
Fides is not always 'bona',
And don't forget to timere Danaos
When they are ferentes their dona.

Bag and baggage, by fair means or foul,
An Englishman's home is his castle,
Of which, simply and solely, in this day and age,
Rack and ruin is part and parcel.

A 'rooted' objection we always express
With neither fear nor favour;
And under misapprehensions
What can we do but labour?

A bottomless pit, a deathly silence –
It's all a crashing bore;
Perhaps we ought to find another
Avenue to explore.

When all's said and done, a breath of fresh air
Would blow the cobwebs away;
By hook or by crook we'll find ways and means,
Hopefully, at the end of the day.

Perhaps, after all, it's up to the poets
Who on language will never renegue:
The last thing you want in a poem's a cliché –
Avoid it like the plague.

Going Up

Like insects from beneath a stone
In University towns,
Creep harassed men with manes of hair
And crumpled suits and frowns,
And pallid youths with acned chins,
Self-conscious in their gowns;

They've all read Kingsley Amis twice
And Brideshead's in their blood;
Whatever tide's in their affairs
They'll take it at the flood,
Determined to be part John Cleese,
Part Levin and part stud.

For the girls up here are a different race
From Sidcup Comprehensive;
More wise, more free, more Virago Press,
More delicately pensive;
More confident, more in demand
And so much more expensive.

Big, confident fish from village ponds
Are lost in this sudden sea,
Where all the doors look all the same
And you're dying for a pee,
And nobody's sure where you go for your grant
Or whether the dinner is free.

And on the official noticeboard
Are lecture lists and courses:
'Prolegomena to Textual Cruces
In Beowulf and its Sources' –
Quite a jump when your last essay
Was 'Ted Hughes' view of Horses'.

So they stroll along the college lawns
Disguising their awe at the quad
Where legions of the famous laughed
And all the great have trod:
Novelists, actors, newsreaders,
Just one step down from God.

And in the Junior Common Room,
With eager and passionate cry,
The debate is on and proud young minds
Demand, with a flash of the eye,
Shall we watch 'Top of the Pops' tonight,
Or shall we see 'Hi-de-Hi'?

So it's back to the ill-lit, draughty room
With walls and shelves all bare
Except for a mug, a revised Roget
And a Good-Luck card from Clare;
To smoke an unpractised cigarette
And start to grow facial hair.

You're dressed in denim, like everyone else;
Like them you've read Joyce, Laurie Lee,
Tolkien, Mervyn Peake, you're an expert on ale,
You talk Labour and vote SDP;
You'll pretend, like the rest, to scorn what you love best –
Oh you're free, you're free, you're free!

Poets' Party

The English Poet Laureates
Are famed for making much
Of victories, inventions,
Royal weddings, births and such;
But in life's small social functions
They're completely out of touch.

So I asked three Poets Laureate
To give us a short burst
Of how they'd cope with putting something
Common into verse.
I gave 'Parties' as the theme, and this
Is Robert Southey first.

Kevin, on a summer's eve
Had locked up the garage
And with spreading belly by the telly
Winced at 'Little and Large';
And by him, like a bird of prey,
Sat Tracey in her negligee.

'Now tell us how the party was!'
Cried Tracy looking coy,
'And why it was you wouldn't take
Me with you - naughty boy!'
Kevin gave a martyred sigh
But answered Tracy by and by.

Meeting and eating
And dancing and prancing
And hopping and bopping
And drinking and winking
And walking and talking
And joking and smoking
And kissing and missing
And lurking and smirking
And clinging and singing
And so on and so forth.

And everybody praised the bloke
Who this great party gave.
'But what good came of it at last?'
Asked Tracy. 'Don't! . . . Behave!'
'Why, that I cannot tell,' said he,
'But 'twas a really great party'

The second Laureate that I asked
I thought might well refuse;
He didn't though, so here it is:
'The Party' by Ted Hughes.

The door swung open. An eyelid. She stood,
Her pale head heavy as metal.
                              Black embers.
Her dress black too; it reminded me
Of a crow; but then –
What doesn't?

Pineapples, pale flesh pierced
With the wooden stake. A plate
Slugged wish sausages. Splinters
Of pig lay on the table, dead.
                    There were other deaths,
Other agonies.
Pale udders of meringue
The rotting fangs of Twiglets,
Bones of bread,
Blood in the cold belly of the glass.

She swallowed an olive – green eye –
As the black earth rips and swallows
Spring.

Gin, white as the snow-fox's grinnning skull
Assuaged our roots.
At morning we staggered home like newts
In the dark lake
Where slippery tons of eggs slide towards birth.
We came
Walloping up roads with the milk wagon.

The last of our three Laureates
But not the least of note,
Is – who else but John Betjeman?
And this is what he wrote:

Gosh, a party! Super-dooper!
Parties are what I like most;
Drinking liquid, Spanish headaches,
Eating small, dead things on toast.

I remember Mabel Oxley's
When I wore my green and white;
Mrs Oxley said 'How grown-up!'
Mr Oxley got quite tight.

Walking down the moonlit garden
Cypresses are tall and cool
Where Mr Oxley loudly vomits
In the ornamental pool.

Do you know he came to see me,
In my room at half-past two;
Asking was I comfy, which was
Quite the sweetest thing to do.

Mrs Oxley came in later,
Now what *was* it that she said?
Something *awfully* funny, such as
'Can we all play blind man's bed?'

Oh, the Oxleys are such poppets –
Both tongue-tied and both so red;
I hope that I'll be just as happy
When I'm fifty-five and wed.

Smarting From Scratch

The Newtown Civic Orchestra
Is not a pretty sight;
Though, compared with what it sounds like
It's a visual delight.
It turns Schumann into cobblers
And Bliss into a blight.

It makes a scant, scorbutic sound,
Wizened, acid, thin:
It's the orchestra that put the 'vile'
Into 'violin';
Where the brass is mostly dominant
Because their tonic's mostly gin.

Sometimes you'll hear a pompous voice
Break the cacophony:
'Why don't we use harmonics here?'
Or 'Let's try this phrase sul G.'
That's Mr Stopes, the leader, dressed
In brief authority;

He teaches history at the tech
And considers himself a pro.
For he had a cup of tea one day
With a man who used to know
The cousin of the second flute
In the Berlin Radio.

The rest of the band are there for different
Reasons. Few can play,
But the ladies are keen on Culture with
An illuminated 'K',
And the gentlemen really fancy themselves
In a nice Moss Bros DJ.

At rehearsals the oboist sits like a stone
And misses all his chances,
Ignoring colleagues' whispers
And the conductor's frantic dances;
He forgot to turn his walkman off
And he's hooked on 'Any Answers'.

Then there's Mrs Tripp – a largo lover,
Andante to the core:
If there's ever a hint of allegro she puts
Her viola on the floor
And takes out Catherine Cookson till
They rall. or rit. once more.

The ensemble and the tuning
Are not quite perfect yet;
The first-desk strings one night played through
The Mendelssohn Octet
And the District Nurse across the road
Went out and called the vet.

A kind of unity comes at times,
There's a prime example of that:
Last orders was called at the pub next door
During Falla's 'Three Cornered Hat,'
And they got from a standstill to prestissimo
In twenty seconds – flat.

But this year, for their concert,
Preparations were unique:
They practised for a month or two
Three evenings every week;
They took their parts home; night by night
They'd scrape and toot and squeak.

And next day in the local rag
For all the world to see
Was the headline: SENSITIVE ACCOUNT
OF PASTORAL SYMPHONY.
A pity, really, since the score
Said 'Mahler No. 3' . . .

'So Foul And Fair A Day
I Have Not Seen'

The local amateur Theatre Group
Put the ache into Ayckbourn – and more:
They murdered Agatha Christie
And they've never been quite Shaw.
This spring they're playing Shakespeare.
They're hoping for a draw.

The play needs the finishing touches now,
Like learning lines and cues;
The costumes are different periods
Which is quite a clever ruse,
But your Warlike Scot is diminished, somewhat,
By the tights and the slip-on shoes.

The flats are over thirty years old,
But still they dazzle the eye;
Well, they would – they're painted in brilliant gloss
And they're not completely dry;
They sag like a freshly-filled nappy and
They wag as the cast walk by.

It's dress-rehearsal night tonight
For 'The Tragedy of Macbeth';
Dustmen, lawyers and barmaids hang
On one another's breath –
Oh, amateur dramatics is
A leveller. Like death.

Macbeth himself is fifty-nine,
But he always gets the lead
Because he's . . . well, he's very good,
He's very good . . . indeed.
And he gave a lot of money when
The company was in need.

His make-up is an orange mask,
Beaded with sweat and stiff;
His eyes so deeply etched with black
It looks almost as if
Two exhausted ravens had flung themselves
Into a sandstone cliff.

King Duncan sits with a drooping fag
Beneath the 'No Smoking' signs
Making paper aeroplanes
From last year's set designs.
The prompter's the only one with nerves –
Well, she'll have most of the lines.

Something's happening to the lights –
The illumination's nil,
And all the cast have wandered off
Knowing there's hours to kill
For, whatever's wrong with the dimmer-board
The electrician's dimmer still.

And in the number three dressing-room
The blonde from the Abbey Life
And the local Co-op manager
Who's playing the Thane of Fife
Are doing . . . some improvisations based
On being man and wife.

There's a telly in the green-room
With the Leichner, crisps and beers
Where snooker addicts learn what drama
Really is, with tears,
And scribble down their entries for
'Shot of the Post-War Years'.

The producer stamps and slams about
With a face like a crumpled bun,
Not because if they started now
They still wouldn't finish till one,
But she just can't seem to command respect
Though she once spoke to Trevor Nunn.

Tempers are frayed, there are tears and sulks
The mascara starts to run;
There are screams from number three dressing-room
Where talk of divorce has begun;
Rows and arguments bubble and boil
But if you ask anyone

Why go through this three times a year?
Why not give up and be done?
They'll all reply, without word of a lie,
'Well, it's such enormous fun!'

Like The Clappers

You listeners to radio,
Have you ever thought at all
As you hear the announcer take his leave
In a voice like a funeral pall,
'Given before an invited audience
In the something-or-other Hall',

Where did the audience come from?
How was it they were found?
Burke's Peerage? A pin and a telephone book?
The geriatrics' bowling-ground?
No – they're just like audiences everywhere
And they make a similar sound.

I know everyone is different
As the truisms all insist,
But there is a law (to actors as true
As Einstein's to a physicist)
That every audience must contain
One each from the following list:

There's the Shuffler, who keeps rearranging his limbs
Or bashing the back of your chair,
Jabbing his programme into your neck
And trapping stray strands of your hair;
Or throbbing his leg through your seat as he en –
Tertains thoughts of the Swedish au pair.

There's the Boozer, who counts up the intervals first
With morose and martyred sigh;
The Nosher, who crunches his way through Act 1
With crisps, barley-sugar, pork pie,
Maltesers – he'll bring out his primus-stove soon
And a packet of bacon to fry.

There's the prof., who's concerned not so much for the play
As to show off his own erudition;
Who talks loudly of Shakespeare's symbol/image schemata
Derived from Peele, Dante and Titian,
And rocks with laughter at all the obscure bits
That baffle the Arden edition.

There's the party of forty who've twice lost their way
And, instead of a journey at leisure,
Arrive in a stew, and they *all* want the loo
And it scarcely increases their pleasure
That they think they've booked for 'The Price is Right'
When it's actually *Measure for Measure*.

There's sometimes the one who looks just like – you know . . .
Whatsisname . . . in that thing on TV!
So the audience gives hardly a glance at the stage
Whispering 'Is it?' . . . 'Don't know,' . . . 'It *must* be!'
And he's in fact a dispensing chemist
From somewhere near Southend-on-Sea.

Last, but not least, there's the Cougher, of course.
I don't cease to be surprised
How attractive the theatre seems to all those
In tubercular demise.
There are 24 types of Theatre Cough
That I've noted and analysed:

There's the scree cough, the free cough
The 'Hey-Mum-this-is-me!' cough;
The boozed cough, the confused cough,
The 'We-Are-Not-Amused' cough;
The curt cough, the pert cough,
The Spray-your-neighbour's-shirt cough;
The bored cough, the assured cough,
The 'Another-hour? Good-Lord' cough;
The head cough, the pre-med. cough,
The kill-the-laugh-stone-dead cough;
The crisp cough, the brisk cough,
That's-something-else-you've-missed cough;
The Gran cough, the Old Man cough,
The Emily, Charlotte and Anne cough;
The neat cough, the discreet cough,
The 'Stone-me-three-quid-a-seat!' cough.

But, of course, these comments don't apply
To present company.
Or do they? If I may coin a phrase
From everyone's mum – 'We'll see . . .'

The Tale of Timothy Greenwich

One dark October the 23rd
In 1948,
In a little Maternity Hospital
Just south of Aldersgate,
Tim Greenwich came into the world
With a cry that cracked a plate;

It broke a neon lighting strip,
A glass of Lucozade,
It put the factory siren well
And truly in the shade;
Men's surgical was just next door –
But damages were paid.

'He's going to be a singer,' said
His mother with a smile;
But no one heard her gently humming
'Music for a While':
For he'd done in both the eardrums
Of the midwife, Mrs Pyle.

His voice broke at the age of twelve,
That's no surprise, you say –
But this child's voice broke everything
That might be in its way;
When other children called they said
'Can Tim come out to slay?'

He'd go out singing Christmas carols
In December's snow;
His 'Silent Night' fused car headlights,
His 'In Dulci Jubilo'
Once killed an aging rector off
And paralysed a crow.

And, as he grew, his voice became
More powerful, less sweet;
His top F# could drop a plane
At 15,000 feet –
The only counter-tenor to make
The Paras look effete.

By 22 he'd realized
He'd never use that voice;
James Bowman or Paul Esswood
Would remain the critic's choice:
His longest job was half an hour
As Stockhausens's 'white noise'.

No concert hall could take the strain
Of him singing publicly,
But on the other hand, he forms
The whole of Chapter Three
In Hans Keller's *Trends in Post-War
Atonality*.

And then, by chance, he strolled into
The BBC one day,
La-la-ing and shattering spectacles,
And he heard somebody say
'Bring me that man immediately
To Studio 7a!'

When he got there, to his utter surprise,
They offered him a show!
And agreed to call it after him
So everyone would know
That he'd made it where it really counts –
On British radio!

And so was born – The Greenwich Time,
And still it's going strong,
And Tim sings out upon the hour
His tinny, timely song –
A harsh and temple-piercing sound:
Five short pips and one long.

Hallowe'en

Oh it's out once again with the face-paints,
The red, the white and the green;
The masks, the cloaks, the rubbery jokes
That border on the obscene,
And all the regalia and paraphernalia
Announcing Hallowe'en.

Oh, the barrow-wights gleam on the outskirts of Cheam,
There are legions of Lamias in Leith;
There are gaggles of ghouls in Hartlepools
And hags on Hampstead Heath;
And warlocks in Porlock will yell through your doorlock
And slide something nasty beneath.

The children arrive at twenty past five
Screaming and ringing the bell;
There are devils galore and ghosts by the score,
Draculas, demons as well;
The costumes admit what we've known for a bit:
The party is going to be hell.

Yes, the coven's convening in dribs and drabs
At 17b The Green,
With growlings and snarlings and 'That'll do, darlings . . .!'
Father retires from the scene
And goes off to read – appropriately –
The current 'Which' magazine.

You'd never think that unattractive child
With his crepe-hair-and-Copydex beard
Could really have genuine magic powers,
But it's certainly very weird:
Auntie Gail put down eight packets of crisps
And every one's disappeared.

And Frankensteins and werewolves
With red, lopsided grin,
Are doing unspeakable things with a candle,
A cat and a nappy-pin;
And a small, persistent, local ghost
Is haunting the biscuit-tin.

The candles inside the pumpkins are lit
With a shrill, bloodcurling chant;
Each turnip glows from mouth and nose
And evil eyes aslant.
One of them looks like Cyril Smith
And the rest like Russell Grant.

But every game's considered too tame;
The indoor fireworks fail;
And no one wants to hear the story
Prepared by Auntie Gail
Who, usually so women's-lib,
Now longs for a fascist male.

The apple-bobbing bowl's been found
And several children dipped;
There are smoky scrawls up the dining-room walls;
The Chippendale's been chipped;
And the carpet's white with stalagmites
Where candle-wax has dripped.

Mother is ragged, perspiring, pink,
But she tries, oh, how she tries!
'I can see the sun's rays! Quick, back to your graves!
All you vampires and ghosts, close your eyes!'
But she still hasn't fed these unlovely undead –
It's a pointless exorcise.

But she gets them through the door at last
And out from under her feet;
They will run amok (with any luck)
In somebody else's street;
And surely the neighbours will have the sense
Always to choose the 'treat'?

There are some real advantages
To these skulls and painted cheeks,
These pointed hats and white-fanged bats
And fake, arterial leaks:
They keep the doorstep free of Jehovah's
Witnesses for weeks.

And kids have played some subtle tricks
At Hallowe'en. Best of all
Was the child who took a mallet and chisel
Down to the churchyard wall
And tapped, with a groan, on an old headstone
In the moonlight's misty pall.

A passer-by heard him tap and sigh
And his skin began to crawl
At that ghostly loom in the midnight gloom
And he leant through the dark to call:
'What are you doing?' The boy replied
'They misspelt my name, that's all . . .'

The Mortgagee's Ode to Winter

Fear no more the heat o' the sun
Here come the winter's rages:
Ninety-odd days of sub-zero gloom –
A re-run of the Dark Ages:
November, December, January,
The Months of the Yellow Pages.

For summer and autumn passed in a haze
Of strawberry teas and fêtes,
When you tried to ignore the rotting front door,
Bad pointing and slipping slates;
But now that the nights are drawing in
The house retaliates.

And when you look at the guttering's sag
And the plaster in the hall,
And the missing stones where the cold wind moans
Through the crumbling larder wall
And your bank statement – you realize
Why autumn was called 'The Fall'.

The experienced among us recognize
That first, fine thrill of dread
When the bland and biddable butter suddenly
Savages the bread;
And breath exhaled in bathrooms stays
And curls about your head;

And cold birds hunch beneath the eaves
Like gloomy caryatids,
And milk-bottles turn to Corinthian columns
Topped with silver lids;
And though you've anti-freezed the car
You have to bump-start the kids.

The central heating takes early retirement,
Squeals like a farrowing pig;
And icicles grow from the overflow
Like a proud, punk, perspex wig;
The bath's full of rust, the Aga has bust,
The loo has gained an 'ig'.

And curtains change colour from bottom to top
As they soak up the seeping rain
That's driven in by each wandering wind
Through the weeping window-pane;
And dampness falls from the flaking walls;
The Axminster's a surrogate drain.

The grinding of loosened roof-tiles goes
With the drip of the downpipe's leak;
There are groans and cricks where the back door sticks,
There's the plumbing's plaintive creak:
The house sounds like the percussion part
From the 'Symphonie Fantastique'.

And you're haunted by paint-stiff, cloth-capped men
Who sigh as they wander through
The musty tomb of each ruined room
On soft, cement-soaked shoe,
And whistle and shake their heads and mutter
'Plus makin' good, that's . . . whoooooh . . .!'

I know a couple who'll go for a year
With never a thought of God,
But when the winter threatens, then
Theology gives a prod
And they'll build a whole religion round
The man from Dyno-Rod.

No, when the outrageous hailstones strike
Like pebbles from a sling;
When nothing in the house will work
But one electric ring;
When the draught from the loft (via Lapland)'s enough
To make your molars sing;

When windows at morning are wasps without warning
(A touch will make them sting);
When plumbers are hibernating and
Won't answer when you ring;
Remember that half-past winter's nearly
Twenty-five to spring.

November the Fifth

November the fifth, and half past one;
The children rush in with a shout
As a tiny cloud goes across the sun –
'It's dark! Can we get them out?'
And Grandmother stirs in her Guinness-dark sleep
With a tiny twinge of gout.

Half-past four, and it's down to the shops –
There's the sausages still to buy;
Her youngest, seeing his Mum distraught,
Flour-flecked and with hair awry,
Slips off his cap and makes 35p
Asking pennies for the Guy.

November the fifth and a quarter to five:
Dirty crockery piled in the sink,
A Matterhorn of grease and glass,
And Mother perspiring and pink;
And then Father comes in with the boss and his wife
For a special Guy Fawkes Night drink . . .

November the fifth and five-fifteen,
And the guests, not expected till six,
Start dribbling in and nibbling at
The quiche and the celery sticks,
And lighting their sparklers and dropping charred ends
In the soup and the cheesecake mix.

November the fifth, and at last it's dark
And the garden is suddenly alive
With anonymous children who trample the beds
Of geranium, fuchsia and chive,
While Father, upstairs, searches wardrobes and drawers
For the fireworks the kids found at five.

Then he's down on his knees among last year's peas
Trying to get the bonfire to go;
And they start without Mum who blows up at the dog
For she can't have a new coat, oh no!
But seven pound fifty can go up in smoke
Every forty-five seconds or so!

November the fifth. Roman candles spit
Shy rockets screech and roar;
And another Catherine wheel gets stuck
On the outside lavatory door,
And the adults are finding it all a hoot
And the children, rather a bore.

November the fifth. Granny's still asleep
Over Mazo de la Roche,
And out in the gloom the bonfire nibbles
At Dad's plastic mackintosh
Which goes up with a 'crump' and adjusts the scene
From Breughel to Hieronymus Bosch.

Then a child coming in for a fresh supply
Of Giant Galactic Fighters
Lets out the dog, who, treading by chance
On some hot pyrotechnic detritus,
Leaves a setter-shaped hole in the larch-lap fence
And a sharp smell of Canis Ignitus.

November the fifth and ten to eleven;
The smiles are wearing down,
And most of the food's trodden into the floor
And the cooker is toffeed and brown,
And everyone's gone by eleven fifteen
To the barbecue at 'The Crown'.

November the fifth and ten to eleven;
Granny wakes. Now what *was* it they said?
There was something special about tonight . . .
Ah, yes! And she nods her head,
And hangs her Christmas stocking up
And toddles off quietly to bed.

The Colonel

I dreamt that out of Guildford I escaped
Down some long, quiet, rhododendron'd lane;
Each shadowed mansion damp and past its prime,
But with a glorious and soul-stirring name –

'Khandi', 'Poonah', 'Khartoum', 'Inkerman',
In faded cream on each old soldier's gate;
Where gardeners' sorties fail to win new ground:
Ivy and elder advance and inspissate.

The autumn tints, the Flames, the Buffs, the Greys,
Are echoes of some unforgotten fight;
And Coldstreams blow through every crumbling lattice
Throughout the long Black Watches of the night.

And Colonel Blainsley-Trutt (Retd.)
Slumps in his leather chair
With a hundred Ghurkas at his feet,
Inniskillins on the stair,
And a couple of Shropshire Light Infantrymen
Snagged in his gun-grey hair.

The careful world that he left by his bed
Somewhere round forty-three,
Its charm, its grace, its British face,
Its predictability,
Has fallen heavily to the floor
And left him with nothing to be.

So he sits by a papier-mâché board,
A self-employed Grim Reaper,
Destroying tin soldiers with trembling hands
Sang-froid and the carpet-sweeper;
He relives at home the attacks at Bapaume
And surveys the carnage at Ypres.

He's fighting Marengo in the hall.
When the trumpet sounds 'retire'
There's always Bosworth Field upstairs,
Or the study with tanks and barbed-wire;
And William and Harold, hammer and tongs
Beside the living-room fire.

Between the bathroom and Waterloo
There's the Battle of Marston Moor;
The kitchen is chaos beneath the strain
Of the Second Punic War:
Hannibal, vegetable and mineral
All mixed up on the floor.

Behind the malted-milk tins lurk
Whole forgotten platoons;
There are King's Hussars in the storage jars
And Fusiliers in the spoons,
And, laid out flat in some rancid fat,
A dozen dead Dragoons.

He strays with rheumy and red-rimmed eyes
Amidst the death and pillage,
Amidst broken crocks and scattered socks
And sour whisky spillage;
Then, with a lift of the spirits, goes
To blast another village.

Of course, toy soldiers cannot scream or bleed;
This is not earnest, no – just harmless fun;
Wars and memories of wars make time recede
Now that the Colonel's occupation's gone.

And when he scatters poppies in Whitehall,
Will they be red or white, this chill November?
For those who fell, or those who could not fall?
Lest he forget, or lest he should remember?

Best Before

I've always been more than faintly suspicious
Of labour-saving machines;
Those smooth and self-effacing
Electronic sci-fi dreams –
You know, six cubic feet of pulsating plastic
Just to chop up a couple of beans.

Oh, they make a Béchamel sauce in four seconds,
Meringues by the dozen for tea,
But putting the things together demands
At least an honours degree;
And six seconds' usage at 12.27
Involves washing up until three.

Now everything follows the same sort of pattern –
Impersonal, clinical, dead;
When you ring up a friend you have to talk
To a chrome cassette instead;
Your entertainment comes out of a box
And nothing comes out of your head.

We've got ways to preserve and ways to destroy,
Clever methods to poison the crops,
And central heating to make us all ill
As soon as the temperature drops;
And, a tiny symptom of all this decay,
Just look at our grocery shops!

Oh, those far-off, halcyon days,
So oft, so long lamented;
When the customer was always right
And the bacon mothball-scented.
And V.A.T. and sell-by dates
Had still not been invented.

When sugar and raisins and almonds came loose
And were scooped into packets of blue;
There was Five Boys Chocolate, the smell of beeswax,
You could buy a farthing chew,
And anything made of Bakelite
Looked slightly parvenu.

And everyone knew who your grandad was
But had never heard of bacteria;
And a purchase included a wise diatribe
On how to prune your wistaria.
No, the 1980's replaced all that
With something highly superior.

Now musak drives you onwards down
The hypermarket's aisle,
As comforting and welcoming
As a corpse with a painted smile,
And slightly less attractive than
A knife on a bathroom tile.

And all the food is hermetically sealed,
Impregnably vacuum-packed
In something like plastic armour-plate
With a date stamped on the back
Which I think is a guess at the date on which
You might manage to get it unwrapped.

There are oranges in plastic nets
That can slice off a nail just like that!
And junk-foods with half-naked girls on the ads –
A real case of tit for tat,
And the trolleys all travel in circles
Like an old, retarded bat.

There are 'home-made' goods whose ingredients
Are nothing but numbers and E's;
There are plastic assistants in plastic coats
Like slices of Edam cheese;
And everyone wears the same expression:
As if they're about to sneeze.

It aspires to be a paradise,
A detergent-scented dream,
But they can't prevent the wild lament
Of the unsweetened toddler's scream
Or bewildered men standing hypnotised
By the jams and the whipping cream.

Oh, où sont les general stores d'antan?
The village grocer? He
And his battered old Austin had some sense
And sensibility;
We need some anachronisms now -
We're so con*temp*orary!

What can we do but cry aloud
'O tempora! O mores';
The musak plays as life decays;
The obvious conclusion to draw is
It's grocers that we have to thank
For Thatcher and her Tories.

Going by the Board

Autumn comes (as autumns will)
And autumn's always the same –
Season of mists and mellow repeats
Of 'I Love Lucy' and 'Fame':
Nothing to challenge the dreadful delight
Of a Family Board Game . . .

Dad brings out the Scrabble with glee:
He's spent the whole of Advent
Memorizing the abstruse words
In the OED Supplement –
And still ends up with words like 'bid'
And 'log' and 'on' and 'went'!

While mother, who's got no competitive spirit
And has played only once before,
Comes out with 'squander', 'exonerate',
'Bequeathed' and 'heretofore'
And remarks such as 'Oh, dear! Is that good?
I've got a triple word score.'

So out comes the Monopoly; that
Takes *real* business acumen:
What to buy and when to sell –
A game for experienced men.
And, as every other year, he'll lose
To his daughter who's just ten.

'You've got to keep open your options,' he smiles
While the game's still going his way.
'Small bits of property all round the board,
Believe me, that's how to play.
Park Lane and Mayfair are tempting, I know,
But you can't hope to make them pay.'

Then he lands on her Mayfair. And then again
And the third time with a hotel.
And he's forced to get rid of his yellows and reds,
Marlborough Street and his stations as well:
He's got mortgaged utilities, twenty-three pounds
And a face like the side of Scafell.

So next the Trivial Pursuit appears.
Now, that *does* depend on knowledge;
The sort that's been gained by a man of the world
Not some clever-dick brat still at college.
An attitude that the next half hour
Is quite long enough to demolish.

Well! . . . 'Who was asleep between Hatter and Hare'!
Who 'exits pursued by a bear'!
If he'd had the questions the others have had,
He'd have won in ten minutes – so there!
It's not what you know, it's the luck of the throw
And the whole thing is grossly unfair.

In Wembley, Kensington, Skirrid and Ludo
He can't do a single thing right;
He's rasher and rasher at Backgammon; Game
Of Life is death tonight;
He's lacking in Scruples; Othello puts out
His light then puts out his light.

And when the police arrive, next day
He's sucking a Mah-Jonng brick
And muttering to himself on the stairs
Wild-eyed, with the hint of a tic:
'It was done by Miss Scarlett in the ballroom
With the rope and the candlestick . . .!'

All the World's a Stage

An actor's life! An actor's life
Is glamorous and free;
A passionate life forever steeped
In British artistry –
Shakespeare, Pinter, Sheridan
And the Social Security.

Your two-hour traffic on the stage
Shows such dichotomy
Between the noblest thoughts of Man,
His richest poetry,
And the cheerless, draughty dressing-room
With its tepid, brick-red tea.

And travelling from Perth to Crewe,
From Kentish Town to Wells,
On a diet of kebab and chips
And Lucozade and Kwells
And, worse than that, two months of nights
In quarter-star hotels.

So when the curtain falls each night
On Venice or Elsinore,
And all the artificial blood's
Been mopped up off the floor,
You find Life's imitated Art
In the Hotel Cockroach d'Or.

Half past ten and the restaurant's closed
And the plastic Tudor creaks
As the wrought-iron lanterns all wink out
In the raffia parrots' beaks
Which have smouldered for hours with electric smells
Like Stilton and parboiled leeks.

So room-service comes, after much delay –
Well, what d'you expect them to do?
They can't face the yellow and turquoise walls
Any more than you;
And to get the lager *quite* that warm
Must take an hour or two.

The radio won't quite turn off
And moans like a sleeping pup;
And the central heating's on full blast
But, push the window up,
And the pipes outside go berserk, and shake
Like dice in a metal cup.

And the en-suite lavatory talks all night
With a sniff and a side-drum roll,
And the rugby forwards in the room next door
Are happily shovelling coal –
I should have believed the neon sign
That said, not HOTEL but HO EL!

So next time an actor fluffs a line,
Remember what he's been through;
With his wife perhaps two hundred miles away
And his kids down with mumps or 'flu,
And he can't get home on an actor's wage
Even *if* the cheque comes through.

Oh! An actor's an artist, a seer, an enchanter,
A weaver of magic spells;
But Guinness or Powell might throw in the towel
After six weeks on tour in hotels!

The Queen's Breakfast

Today is the Opening of Parliament –
That home of legalized malice
Which combines all the charm of John McEnroe
With the cultural content of 'Dallas';
The Queen will be there at eleven: just now
It's breakfast time at the Palace.

It isn't so hard to imagine the scene,
The Queen's only human like us,
She's got to be up to be sure of the coach
Or it's all on the 42 bus,
And she hasn't applied for her pensioner's pass
And those fare-boxes *are* such a fuss.

And over her breakfast, in curlers and slippers,
It's decision time again –
Not just between jam and peanut-butter
(The crunchy or the plain)
But could she smuggle a crossword into
The House beneath her train?

Will she finish by lunch, or should she leave Phil
Some moussaka in a pan?
Could she wear something off the shoulder to show
Her Carribean tan?
Does she dare to address the House of Lords
And the Commons with 'Hey, Man!'

'And what,' she asks, 'will the music be?'
Says the Duke, 'Oh, don't be a chump, it's
Always the same, year in, year out,
(Be an angel and pass the crumpets)
One of those Malcolm Williamson things
For twenty-six ill-tempered trumpets.

But what can the country be thinking of?
She's only just back from her cruise
And they expect her to write up an opening speech,
Well – an old one might be better news;
Or else, having paid him his barrel of sack,
Let's get something out of Ted Hughes?

So – into the carriage and out on the road,
And her speech is still not done;
And she thinks as she chews her pencil, this will
Be no problem at all for her son:
He can do his endless Goon impressions
Of Eccles and Henry Crunn.

But with Thatcher and Kinnock and Owen and Steel
All poised for the fray, how does one
Phrase an address to Parliament?
It must be appropriately done.
So she jots down, at last, the end of her speech,
It reads: 'Seconds out – Round one!'

The Twelve Signs of Christmas

You know by the shriek of the siren
That the bomb is going to fall;
You know when the cat's been locked in all day
By the smell in the entrance hall;
When the Arab sees dust on the distant dunes
He knows that a sandstrom's near,
And when Christmas approaches in England,
The signs are just as clear.

The very first sign, not long after dawn,
On a day with no breath of a breeze,
Is a sound as of twelve dozen bison gripped
By a terminal lung disease;
And the cars up the street can't get to their feet
And their owners are all on their knees,
And the pavement is littered with hair-driers, kettles,
And – too late! – the anti-freeze.
The second sign is a sign of *The Times*,
Or perhaps the *Observer* instead;
It involves a very long list of books,
Not one of which you've read,
Chosen by writers as being the ones
That went furthest over their head
And designed to show the rest of us
That we're intellectually dead.
The third is the sign of the *Radio Times*
Which suddenly triples its size
And sports sundry tasteless ribbons and bells,
While newsreaders in festive guise
Sing carols in polystyrene snow,
And TV stars tell lies
About their childhoods, and someone talks

To Wogan – now there's a surprise.
The fourth sign is called The Change of Heart
Where parcels, once squashed flat
Or left to soak up rain all day,
Land gently on the mat;
And first-class letters arrive on time
And the postman tips his hat
And smiles, the model of genial warmth,
Hoping you'll tip for tat.
The fifth is the sudden plethora
(There's one every time you blink)
Of 'X' certificate films that warn us
Not to drive and drink.
The sixth is the programme that teaches you how
To cloak any alcohols's stink
And how to imbibe twice as much as is safe
And still not end up in clink.
The seventh's the cotton-wool that disgraces
Every bow-windowed shoppe;
The eighth is the hair-of-the-dog advice
That Kingsley Amis will drop;
The ninth is the latest Christmas carol
All pap combined with pop;
The tenth is the realization that
It's gone too far to stop.
The eleventh is the weatherman
Who's sorry that he can't fix
A proper white Christmas again this year,
But the Beeb will show Crosby flicks . . .
And the twelfth is that lorry draws to a halt
On Christmas Eve at six;
It has come to replenish the empty shops –
With Easter eggs and chicks.

The Christmas Horrortorio
or
Quittez Shoppeurs

Angels from the realms of glory
Sing the angel strain:
God help you, merry gentlemen,
It's Christmas time again;
Lo, Mammon's in the manger now
And Purse has come to reign.

A cold coming we had of it,
A wettish coming, too;
With third-hand slush in a wet, brown mush
Folding over the shoe;
And everyone else has more to spend
And less to buy than you.

And your eardrums sing with the north wind's sting
And the four-year-old's spoilt soprano;
And all the gift-shop windows are sprayed
With artificial guano.
It's Christmas shopping time once more:
Mens santa in Co-op insano.

About this time of the year, of course,
The shops stay open later:
More time to scurry like frantic ants
From grocer to toyshop to baker
With your sleeve being tugged and your privates mugged
By rolls of wrapping paper.

And the list you've carefully marshalled over
Weeks of inspiration
Takes a sudden dive into
The local irrigation
And comes out quite unreadable, like
Some Sanskrit chant-notation.

'Tailless voles' could be 'Toilet rolls'
And 'Frobfast' is 'Food for cat';
'Farters in slips' must be 'Packets of crisps';
Is that 'Wombat' or 'Woolly hat'?
And what on earth is 'Prulid twenn'?
Or 'Wyxtog' or 'Ghengis Pratt'?

The Salvation Army silver band,
With harmony slightly aslant,
Makes a sound like a plush chaise-longue in song
By the Oakleaf Restaurant,
But they see amid the winter's snow
What many of us can't.

And battling through a vicious queue
For a festive biscuit-jar,
Or jostling the hollies and lethal brollies
Or loading up the wrong car,
You suddenly realize where they shot
The stills for *A Bridge Too Far*.

And any Christmas spirit you had
Exhaustedly expires
In a welter of tinselled, tawdry shops
Awash with boozy buyers,
And endless sleazy, sentimental,
Syncopated choirs.

There are clothes, books, discs, dolls, games, plants, toys
And foodstuffs enough to choke on;
But when you find just what you're looking for
There's only one left – and it's broken;
So it's after-shave again, or a tie,
Or a W. H. Smith token.

There are merry mugs and diaries
And merry napkin-rings,
And all the sad variety
Of useless Yuletide things
Displayed with ghastly gaucherie
And origami Kings.

And amid the glitter, the slush, the crush,
The streetcorner body-popping,
The drunks, the manic emptorial panic,
The money-for-old-rope swapping,
'Noel' sing we all. And you agree,
There's no 'ell like Christmas shopping.

Psalm CLI

1. Give ear, O LORD, unto my cry that goeth not out of feigned lips: for Christmas is nigh, and my bank balance is as scarlet.
2. My relations compass me about, and the noise of commercials is heard in the land: O LORD my God, let me not be consumed.
3. 'Consumed?' saith the LORD, 'It is thou wilt do the consuming if I know thee: and I, the LORD thy God, am omniscient in case thou hadst forgotten.'
4. And in my anguish I called again unto the LORD: and he answered me and said, 'Oh, thou callest upon me now, dost thou? That is big of thee! And when my birthday cometh, that is CALLED Christmas, wilt thou so much as wish me many happy returns?'
5. O, give ear and hear me, for this is how Christmasses shall be from this day forth.
6. Thine in-laws shall come from the east and from the west, yea, from the uttermost parts of the earth: bath-cubes shall they bring, talc also and much cheap bubble-bath, K-Tel records, Malibu, Charles and Di keyrings, car deodorants, soap-on-a-rope and a shaggy cover for the lid of the loo.
7. The high hills are a refuge for the wild goats, but from Sharon's ghetto-blaster shall there be no refuge: Kevin shall play upon his untuned cymbals, yea, upon his loud cymbals.
8. Auntie Alice shall be for an affliction unto thee, playing 'Jingle Bells' with one finger upon the Hammond Organ: her knitting hath been going on for months, and thou shalt be covered with a garment as with the deep.
9. The turkey also shall burn, and the smoke thereof shall make a mess of the Laura Ashley: small but tone-deaf

149

carol singers shall be from everlasting to everlasting.

10. The milkman shall be hung over, and shall be mindful of the earful thou gavest him when he trod on thy trailing lobelia: therefore shall he naff off early and forget your special order.

11. There shall be Family Games, for, lo, the telly will be on the blink: yet will I the LORD restore vision unto the telly, but only for the duration of 'Little and Large'.

12. Then shalt thou resort to drink, yea, to very much strong drink: for I, the LORD, have hidden the not-to-be-missed feature films from thee, and a day is as a thousand ages in thy sight.

13. And in the watches of the night, with groaning and gnashing of the teeth shalt thou steer the porcelain bus: and thy twelve-year-old malt, which thou hiddest beneath the sink, shall be mistaken for Dettol.

AMEN.

Breaking the News

Twelfth night is past, the season's done,
The decorations fall;
The tree has scored its usual gash
Along the living-room wall,
And the last Christmas card arrived just now
From somewhere near Nepal.

The carpet's a kind of palimpsest
Of all that the season's been,
It bears contributions from baby, cat,
Pine-needles, sellotape, gin;
And that vile, unidentifiable lump
The first-footer trampled in.

So, how has it been? A hundred films
With built-in obsolescence;
The songs one sings for obscure Kings
Who do silly things with peasants;
The numinous sense of vast expense
And, yes – oh yes – the presents!

The Swedish glass from Auntie Nan
Arrives in forty pieces;
The liquid patch beneath the tree
Is a selection of French cheeses;
The Hockney print has six sharp, deep,
Ineradicable creases.

The candle-making kit's resolved
Itself into a jelly
And seeped through all interstices
And put paid to the telly;
The indestructible boomerang broke
On contact with Aunt Nellie.

The torch's beam is a dullish gleam
If you swear and thump and shake it;
The cogs and wheels make plastic squeals
In the Fisher-Price 'Learn and Play' Kit;
The bed-head lamp has snapped from its clamp:
The Cointreau didn't make it.

The new computer software tapes,
By some mental aberration,
Were wiped clean trying to record
The Queen's Speech to the Nation;
And Granny's wheelchair soon saw off
The Lego Moonbase station.

The Japanese goldfish Abigail showered
With turkey, chocolate and bread;
She boiled up a kettle and filled his bowl
'To keep him warm in bed . . .'
He's floating belly upwards now –
'Ooh, isn't he *clever*!' she said.

The musical box played 'Greensleeves' twice
And now plays 'G★★ens★ee★★★';
The robot dinosaurs were left
On the cooker, during tea,
And melted their micro-circuits into
The turkey fricassee.

But there are things that Christmas brings
Impossible to break:
No moving parts, no batteries
No glass, no mess to make.
It's nice to know there's something
Christmas-proof, for goodness sake!

'Venetian Scene: 1000 pieces
Fully interlocking'
Was what young Richard pulled with glee
From a bulging Christmas stocking.
Now he's fitted nine hundred and ninety-nine . . .
And the baby won't stop coughing . . .

A Day to Remember

The British love their heritage,
Their pomp and pageantry;
And nothing suits them better than
An anniversary –
An excuse for a toast and a flag on a pole,
Or a plaque, or to plant a tree.
Every day of the year belongs to a saint
Or a much more colourful sinner:
Someone died, or someone was born
King Alfred burnt the dinner,
Or something remarkable happened, or
The West Indies brought on a spinner.
But the dullest day in all the year
Is the nineteenth of February,
For nothing of note took place today
As far as I can see,
And it's time we did something about it
And gave it identity.
So – let's make it a day when we celebrate
The oddest and worst that has been –
Whatever you like that's not already
Kept its memory green
We'll think of and drink to every year
On dull old Feb. nineteen.
It's the day of St Aloysius Lepp,
Patron saint of hopeless cases
Who turned too fast from temptation
And was strangled in his braces;
The day they invented nappy-rash,
Earwax and empty spaces.
It's the day on which David Coleman made sense,
And Cannon and Ball told jokes;

154

The day they discovered that Milton Keynes
Was just an elaborate hoax;
It's National Scum and Tidemark day,
And, in 356 B.C.
Hats were invented; the first was worn
At twenty-five past three.
It's National Flag-day Flag-day today;
And comments about the weather
Were first passed in England on Feb. the nineteenth,
And the Scots invented heather.
The day of the first known incidence
Of musak in restaurants;
It's a day to rejoice because square things don't roll
And Frenchmen live in France.
The Greeks were invented, and Income Tax,
Barry Manilow sang in tune,
And someone invented fluffy dice
To hang in the family saloon.
It's the day they passed the law that says
Whichever queue you decide on
Will be the slowest moving;
And it's one that can be relied on.
On February the nineteenth
Latin became a dead language;
The cabinet stayed intact all day;
B.R. used the first welded sandwich.
But how to commemorate such a great day?
Have a party? Or write an encomium?
Monks can stay in and celibate
Round the monastery harmonium;
I suggest we observe – at 11 o'clock –
Two minutes' pandemonium.

The Society For Poor English

An Ode, today, for English words
Whose meanings are lost in the mists
Breathed by commentators, clots,
And jobbing journalists

Who can't see any difference
Between dis- and un- interested,
Blackmail and threat, fewer, less,
Refute, deny – instead

They bellow out their ignorance
For all the world to see,
And like it or not, we're victims of
Linguistic larceny.

You may not think it matters much,
But look at where it lands you:
You use a word precisely, now,
And nobody understands you.

Well, don't despair, but join me in
My plan to intervene
With words that don't exist, but should.
I'll tell you what I mean.

It came to me the other day
When reading some abstruse book,
And I came across this word 'un-derfed';
I took another look.

'Un*derf*ed?' I thought. 'What is this verb
To derf?' I scratched my head.
'Underfed, underfed . . .' and then it clicked –
'Un*derf*ed?' no – 'under*fed*'!

And then I thought, 'There's lots of words
That one could find like this,
That sound as if they're negatives
Starting un- or de- or dis-.'

Remove from them their prefixes
And you get a brand-new word;
Look dainfully upon them,
However struse or surd.

You hear of people demolishing or
Dismantling a wall;
But of buildings molished or mantled
You hardly hear at all.

But here are two quite useful terms,
Lexical gems, I'd say;
We must pute and parage them while they're funct,
They'll help the language cay.

You must always turb a sleeping dog,
So the proverb goes;
Well, he won't be very gruntled if
You kick him in the nose.

A crowd can be dispersed, dismissed,
But, under this new system,
If you want to bring them back again
You simply perse and miss them.

To make up quantities again
There's a useful word – to plete;
And if you can't keep a secret
Presumably you're creet.

To 'ceive' must mean to tell the truth
But the words I like the best
Are those that signify peace of mind:
Mented, traught and tressed.

Not being a parent's brother
Is a state known as 'cle'; and perforce,
When you *do* have a nephew or niece,
Well, then you're an 'uncle', of course.

Oh English words, you English words!
Hevelled, kempt and couth;
Ruly, gainly and always descript,
And crepit with lasting youth.

I can see how poets get drunk on words,
But that's not true of me:
I'm ebriate, generate, quite solute,
And as bauched as bauched can be.